Entrepreneurship, Intrapreneurship, and Venture Capital

Entrepreneurship, Intrapreneurship, and Venture Capital

The Foundation of Economic Renaissance

Edited by
Robert D. Hisrich
The University of Tulsa

Lexington Books
D.C. Heath and Company/Lexington, Massachusetts/Toronto

Library of Congress Cataloging-in-Publication Data

Entrepreneurship, intrapreneurship, and venture capital.

  Contents: Importance of entrepreneurship in economic development / Howard H. Stevenson and William A. Sahlman—Role of entrepreneurship in economic development / Donald L. Sexton—Building indigenous companies / Raymond W. Smilor—[etc.]
   1. Entrepreneur—Addresses, essays, lectures.
2. Venture capital—United States—Addresses, essays, lectures.   I. Hisrich, Robert D.
HB615.E634 1986   338'.04   85-45519
ISBN 0-669-11867-2 (alk. paper)

Published simultaneously in Canada
Printed in the United States of America
Casebound International Standard Book Number: 0-669-11867-2
Library of Congress Catalog Card Number: 85-45519

The paper used in this publication meets the minimum requirements of American National Standard for Information Sciences—Permanence of Paper for Printed Library Materials, ANSI Z39.48-1984.

The last numbers on the right below indicate the number and date of printing.

10 9 8 7 6 5 4 3 2 1

95 94 93 92 91 90 89 88 87 86

Dedicated to Jerry L. Hudson, President, Edward F. Keller, Chairman and CEO, and all at the Fourth National Bank of Tulsa who were "entrepreneurial enough" to sponsor an unproven seminar.

Contents

Figures and Tables

Figures

Tables

Preface

Governmental units, business leaders, and citizens have shown increasing interest in the economic development and economic growth of their areas. No matter how great that interest, though, there frequently is misunderstanding regarding the terms *economic development* and *economic growth* as well as the methods for accomplishing economic well-being for their particular area of concern. Although similar, the two terms are not identical. Growth may be necessary but not sufficient for development. Economic growth refers to increases in a country's production or income per capita, with the economy's total output of goods and services usually being measured by gross national product (GNP). Economic development, on the other hand, goes beyond economic growth to include changes in output distribution and economic structure, which may affect such things as improvement in the material well-being of the less fortunate, technical advances, increased manufacturing, construction, and finance in the GNP of the area, and increases in the education level. Economic development refers not only to the rate of change in economic well-being but also its level.

What causes growth and economic development of an area? The factors contributing to growth can be visualized by examining the contributing elements to production: labor, natural resources, technology, capital, and entrepreneurship. Labor refers to the skills and number of individuals possessing each skill in an area. For certain types of production to occur, it is necessary that certain skill levels are present. Natural resources are, of course, a heterogeneous grouping of the resources of an area. Although the supply of natural resources is important, of even more importance is the availability through the flow into an area. The third element—technology—refers to the level of skills, knowledge, and procedures for producing certain types of goods and services. For example, an area that has the technology available to produce computers and peripheral equipment will tend to develop and attract more firms in these businesses than an area that does not. Capital refers to the availability of cash as well as plant, equipment, machinery, and buildings. Where capital is available, an area develops economically and new businesses form. New business formation is the result of the final contributing element—entrepreneurship. Entrepreneurship is the production resource that coordinates the other four elements—labor, natural resources, technology, and capital. As such, the entrepreneur is the innovator and coordinator so necessary for the economic development of an area.

The rapid economic growth of the United States is basically a story of the discovery and adoption of novel and improved ways of satisfying wants and needs. These wants and needs have been satisfied by such captains of industry as J. P. Morgan (finance), James B. Duke (tobacco), Andrew Carnegie (steel), Cornelius Vanderbilt (railroads), and John D. Rockefeller (oil). In each of these instances the innovation process took place: a new idea or invention was commercialized. All too frequently, new ideas or inventions are developed that are not needed or that fail to obtain a sponsor, funding, or a market necessary for commercialization.

The economist who links this innovation process to the entrepreneur is Joseph A. Schumpeter. Schumpeterian economics maintains that successful innovation brings about economic growth in an area and is the source of private profits. According to Schumpeter the entrepreneur is the driving force behind this growth, formulating new economic combinations by (1) developing new markets; (2) developing new sources of materials; (3) accumulating capital resources in a new area; (4) introducing new products and new production functions; and (5) reorganizing or developing a new industry.[1]

Despite Schumpeter's economic theory, there has been a lack of understanding and an inability to translate it into action in many areas of the United States, which is the purpose of this book. The book grew from a well-received seminar in the Tulsa, Oklahoma, area that was sponsored by the Fourth National Bank of Tulsa. Participants in this seminar as well as individuals elsewhere indicated a need to have the concepts and suggestions further developed and enumerated in print.

The book contains three parts, each with two chapters. The first part, *Impact of Entrepreneurship on Economic Development,* with chapters by Howard Stevenson and William Sahlman and by Donald Sexton, deals with the issue of entrepreneurship and economic development. In chapter 1, Howard Stevenson and William Sahlman discuss the resurging interest in and the magnitude of entrepreneurship in the United States. After discussing some of the behavioral and historical issues in the field, Stevenson and Sahlman conclude the chapter by comparing the manager versus the entrepreneur on several critical dimensions: strategic orientation, commitment of resources, control of resources, and concept of management structure. Donald Sexton, in chapter 2, builds on Stevenson's and Sahlman's ideas by discussing the concept of economic growth and the factors affecting new venture initiation and growth. Sexton concludes with an analysis of the impact of local initiatives on this new venture creation.

Part II, *Role of New-Company Creation in Economic Development,* focuses on the aspects of building indigenous companies and expanding existing ones to facilitate the economic renaissance of an area. Raymond Smilor provides several different models an area can use to develop technology ventures in light of the hypercompetition within industries and between areas for attracting companies or helping them to grow. Concepts such as incubators and the entrepreneurial network are explored. In addition, Smilor discusses trends in economic development and describes selected university–corporation programs presently operating throughout the United States. Robert Hisrich extends Smilor's concepts of product evolution and the product planning and development process. The role of government, intrapreneurship, and entrepreneurship in this development process is discussed along with mechanisms that make intrapreneurship and entrepreneurship have a positive impact on the economic development of an area.

Part III, *Role of Venture Capital in Economic Development,* addresses the important topic of financing an economic renaissance. In chapter 5, Barry Davis examines the role of venture capital in this process. The chapter looks at the role of the venture capital industry in the United States and the types of venture capital concerns. The philosophy, objectives, and process of a venture capital firm are examined along with the method by which an entrepreneur obtains venture capital funding. William Wetzel, in the final chapter, addresses a very specialized segment of risk capital markets—the informal risk capital market. The nature and scope of the participants in this market are described as well as a unique method—the Venture Capital Network—for facilitating the active participation of this market in the economic renaissance of an area.

This book should be read by anyone interested in the economic revitalization, growth, and development of an area: members of chambers of commerce, economic planners, urban developers, bankers, real estate developers, businesspeople, and every concerned citizen. The process, although complex, is one that can be readily understood and incorporated into the public policy of an area.

Many people have helped make this book possible: the authors, who took time from their busy schedules to write their respective chapters; Charlotte Wilson, who typed the manuscript; Jerry L. Hudson and Edward F. Keller of the Fourth National Bank of Tulsa, which sponsored the original seminar; and Bruce Katz, who made helpful editorial comments. I am particularly indebted to my wife, Tina, and children, Kelly, Kary, and Katy, whose patience, support, encouragement, understanding, and love helped bring this effort to fruition.

Notes

1. Schumpeter's economic theory and the Schumpeterian model can be found in Joseph A. Schumpeter, *The Theory of Economic Development* (New York: Oxford University Press, 1961), pp. 95–156.

Part I
Impact of Entrepreneurship on Economic Development

1

Importance of Entrepreneurship in Economic Development

Howard H. Stevenson
William A. Sahlman

T he word *entrepreneurship* has entered the managerial vocabulary as the 1980s' equivalent of *professionalism,* the managerial buzzword of the 1970s. Managers are trying to understand the concept of entrepreneurship and how their own organizations can be made more *entrepreneurial.* As might be expected, a phalanx of consultants and advisors has entered the market to help managers accomplish the goal of instilling entrepreneurship in their companies.

Our purpose in this chapter is to offer an explanation for the extraordinary level of interest in the topic of entrepreneurship. First, we document the increase in the incidence of entrepreneurship and in the degree of public awareness and interest in the phenomenon. Then, we offer a definition of entrepreneurship as a process of management. On the basis of this definition, we suggest why we believe encouraging entrepreneurial behavior is critical to the long-term vitality of the U.S. economy. Most importantly, we show that the practice of entrepreneurship is as important, if not more important, to large, mature companies as it is to the high technology start-ups that many observers describe as the sole repositories of entrepreneurial behavior. Entrepreneurship is not a fad; even if some of the more visible indicators of interest ebb, the necessity of continued focus on entrepreneurship by managers and academics will continue unabated.

Resurgent Interest in Entrepreneurship

For years entrepreneurship has been regarded as a stage through which organizations passed on their way to good management and success. Few schools, almost no large-sized companies, and very few managers considered the development of entrepreneurship to be an appropriate goal. This has changed. There are signs on many fronts of interest in entrepreneurship. The magnitude of interest is remarkable and the research being carried out in the entrepreneurial domain has become significant. The entrepreneurial energy being applied to entrepreneurship is a phenomenon in and of itself.

Signs of an Entrepreneurial Revolution

The entrepreneurial revolution has not arrived unnoticed. Evidence of interest is available on many fronts—journalistic, managerial, economic, political, and educational—and is pointing to broad recognition of problems for which diverse groups have identified *entrepreneurship* as the solution. Later we infer the problem to which entrepreneurship seems to be the solution, but first we examine the evidence of interest.

Journalistic evidence of interest in entrepreneurship abounds. Covers of the basic business journals *Fortune, Business Week, Forbes, Nations Business,* and *Dun's* have all featured profiles of entrepreneurs and entrepreneurial firms. The pictures of Apple Computer's Steve Jobs, Lotus Development's Mitch Kapor, People Express's Don Burr, among others, have been featured as they led the spectacular growth of their respective organizations. The success chronicles have been displayed prominently with praise and awe of the accomplishments shining through. These firms, which are small relative to those normally featured, were highlighted and explored.

Beyond the standard business journals, new and specialized magazines devoted solely to entrepreneurship have sprung up. Bernard Goldhirsch's *INC.* and Joseph Giaraputto's *Venture* take serious aim at the entrepreneur by providing articles that give advice, information, and solace. Founders of firms discovered that they were not suffering problems alone. Their entrepreneurial successes were tabulated and chronicled in the *INC.* and *Venture* 100's and 500's. These magazines became huge commercial successes. For those entrepreneurs not yet past the starting stage, *Entrepreneur* and *In Business* focus on identifying opportunities and providing a push to get going.

The daily press marked the emergence of entrepreneurship as well. The *Wall Street Journal* features a weekly small business column as well as having run a special section on entrepreneurship. The *New*

York Times has acknowledged entrepreneurship in its business section, its "op ed" section, and even in the book review section. Entrepreneurship and entrepreneurs have become news.

Book publishers have also recognized the market. The success of *In Search of Excellence* opened the floodgates for new books about innovative firms, creative management, and the entrepreneur. The histories of individual entrepreneurs have been chronicled, the "how to" books have proliferated, and the textbook market has exploded.

In addition to journalistic evidence, the world of big business has indicated that whatever entrepreneurship may be, more of it is needed. The president of General Electric has announced an entrepreneurial mission for the multibillion dollar giant he leads; Exxon, the world's largest company, created (and later disbanded) a new venture group. IBM created and successfully managed a start-up Entry Systems Division to launch its Personal Computer. Other firms, such as Sohio, Analog Devices, and Monsanto, have created venture capital investment vehicles to enable them to support entrepreneurship outside of the traditional structures.

Consultants also have signed on to the surge in entrepreneurial interest. Many consulting firms have moved from being entirely focused on strategy consulting to focusing on innovation. For example, McKinsey and Company, the international management consulting firm, encouraged two partners to join up with members of the American Business Conference to study the characteristics of America's midsize growth companies. Small is not necessarily beautiful, but the giants of industry acknowledge both publicly and privately that many of the features of small entrepreneurial firms make them formidable competitors and such features must be introduced into the big firms if they are to survive and prosper.

The economists also have begun to acknowledge the importance of the entrepreneurial function based on their data. In all countries in which job creation has been carefully studied, economists have found that small, entrepreneurial firms have been disproportionately responsible for job creation. The U.S. government reported in *The State of Small Business: A Report of the President* that for various periods between 1972 and 1982 small businesses responded more quickly to market opportunities and created more than their proportionate share of new jobs as part of that response. The seminal work of David Birch at MIT first pointed out this fact. The U.S. government report found that small business dominated industries added jobs at a rate almost twice that of industries dominated by larger firms: 11.4 percent compared to only 5.3 percent from November 1982 through October 1984. That same report emphasized that "67 percent of all new jobs in this country are created by small business and that small firms account for 38 percent of the Gross National Product."

Taking the lead from Birch's original U.S. studies, researchers in England, Holland, and many lesser-developed countries have found similar results. Small, entrepreneurial firms are leading in the economic creation of wealth and jobs.

These studies have not gone unnoticed by politicians. A survey by the accounting firm Touche Ross revealed that 82 percent of the mayors of more than half of the cities of 250,000 or more population believed small business to be more important in job creation than large firms.

Another striking phenomenon is the emergence of interest in entrepreneurship at universities. The number of courses offered in entrepreneurship has increased eightfold over the last nine years according to a survey done by Karl Vesper. The content of the courses has changed and additional research has been done. Harvard's President, Derek Bok noted this trend when he said:

> The [Harvard] Business School is beginning to see its role is not just training general managers but also to train and provide a preparation for people starting their own business. . . . It's a kind of a new freedom to go out and take some risks and run your own show . . . it's a kind of a new frontier for people of some boldness and creativity.

Endowed chairs in entrepreneurship have been created at over fifteen institutions. Alumni interest is high; Harvard has received funding for five chairs in the field. Educational institutions are responding by developing in-house expertise, recruiting experienced entrepreneurs as adjunct faculty, and motivating existing faculty to extend their research and teaching domains.

Increasing Incidence of Entrepreneurship

By any measure, the rate of business start-ups has increased. During the past thirty years, the number of new businesses started has in-

Table 1–1
Trend in New Securities Issues Market, 1975
to 1984

Year	Number of Issues	Total Value ($000,000)
1975	203	$ 1,257
1976	229	1,265
1977	216	2,167
1978	244	3,100
1979	288	3,585
1980	584	8,623
1981	998	14,659
1982	813	10,694
1983	1,589	25,312
1984	1,411	20,065

Source: *Small Business Financing Trends 1975–1984*
(U.S. Securities and Exchange Commission, Directorate
of Economic and Policy Analysis, 1985).

creased from ninety-three thousand annually to well over six hundred
thousand. Self-employment has increased by 25 percent during the
same period.

One indirect indicator of the increase in entrepreneurship has been
the market for initial public offerings of securities. The Directorate of
Economic and Policy Analysis of the U.S. Securities and Exchange
Commission (SEC) recently prepared an analysis of new issues of securities. The number and magnitude of initial public offerings is an
important measure of market support for new and untried ideas. Table
1–1 shows the trend in the new issues market from 1975 to 1984.

Increased interest was also reflected in the way in which the stock
was placed with the public. Whereas in 1975 almost all small company initial public offerings were done directly by the company, by
1984 over 75 percent of the initial public offerings were underwritten
by an investment banker or done on the basis of a professionally managed best-efforts offering. Moreover, initial public offerings accounted
for only 3 percent of the total registered offerings in 1975 and for over
25 percent in 1983.

These trends are mirrored in the venture capital markets. The de-

Table 1–2
Venture Capital Industry Funds
(thousands of dollars)

Year	Net New Private Capital Committed to Venture Capital Firms	Size of Total Pool	Estimated Disbursements to Portfolio Companies
1984	$4,200	$16,300	$3,000
1983	4,500	12,100	2,800
1982	1,800	7,600	1,800
1981	1,300	5,800	1,400
1980	700	4,500	1,100
1979	300	3,800	1,000
1978	600	3,500	550
1977	39	2,500–3,000	400
1976	50	"	300
1975	10	"	250
1974	57	"	350
1973	56	"	450
1972	62	"	425
1971	95	"	410
1970	97	"	350
1969	171	"	450

Source: Venture Economics, Inc., Wellesley, Massachusetts.

Notes: Net new private capital = total new private capital less withdrawals. All numbers measured at cost.

cade 1975–1984 saw explosive growth. Table 1–2 shows the amount invested in venture funds during this period. Although the magnitude of initial public offerings and venture capital assets is small relative to total investment capital of the United States, the trends indicate increasing economic importance.

With the increasing economic significance of entrepreneurship has come increasing political involvement and clout. Annual meetings of the SEC Business Government Commission on Access of Small Business to Capital have been held since 1981. A White House Conference on Small Business was held in 1980 with another scheduled for 1986. New and relatively effective lobbying efforts have been mounted for tax, purchasing, and tariff protection for small business. There often

Table 1–3
Papers Submitted at Babson Conference on Entrepreneurship Research

Year	Papers Submitted	Authors
1981	39	59
1982	35	58
1983	37	60
1984	43	67
1985	60	97

is considerable confusion in the minds of politicians between small business and entrepreneurial businesses, although, as will be seen, the economic distinction is both real and important.

Expansion of the Research Base

The present wave of interest in entrepreneurship is not the first. Under the leadership of Joseph Schumpeter and Arthur Cole, Harvard's Center for the Study of Entrepreneurship was a wellspring of important research during the 1940s. Though this effort was disbanded in 1946, it left a major impact in the form of a thriving group of business history scholars, including Alfred D. Chandler, Arthur Cole, and Ralph Hidy, among others.

More recent efforts in entrepreneurial research have proceeded on a different basis. Scholars from academic disciplines ranging from psychology to business administration to economics have contributed new research. The result has been an explosion in papers, books, and doctoral dissertations. It is interesting to note the progression in papers submitted to the Babson Conference on Entrepreneurship Research. Table 1–3 shows this growth. Even the 1985 Strategic Management Conference, a setting not known for interest in this subject, had almost 10 percent of its papers dealing with entrepreneurial subjects. Many of the traditional outlets for publication of academic research are publishing material on entrepreneurship, including *The Harvard Business Review, Sloan Management Review, Management Science,* and the *Journal of the Academy of Management.*

Why is Entrepreneurship Important?

The interest in entrepreneurship seems to be broad-based. The present surge in activity appears to derive from at least four sources. First, only recently have the data that testify to the economic importance of entrepreneurship become widely disseminated. As this has occurred, additional attention has been given to the ideologic foundations of the entrepreneurial economy. Entrepreneurship has also come to be viewed as the dominant strength of the United States in its international competitive battle. Finally, there is the overwhelming evidence that, for groups comparable in background and education, those who are self-employed entrepreneurs find more satisfaction in their jobs. These four bases—economic, chauvinistic, ideological, and psychological—merit further exploration, but the evidence is already accumulating.

Economic Importance of Entrepreneurship

The dramatic increase in the incidence of new business formation has had a major impact on the way people work. The number of self-employed has grown by over 20 percent from 1970 to 1980 according to official census data. An additional 1.5 million individuals became self-employed during that decade.

Increased attention on entrepreneurship has also been sparked by the evidence gathered by David Birch that medium and smaller companies supplied almost three-quarters of the new jobs created. Birch also found that between 12 percent and 15 percent of the smaller firms accounted for the vast majority of all new job creation.[4] One consequence of this process is that almost 70 percent of all employees work for companies employing less than 250 people.

The message from Birch is that the engines of change are small and select, and we must gain a better understanding of those small but effective economic units. This conclusion has been replicated in many other countries. Economists have learned that the predictions of leading economists regarding the demise of the entrepreneur were indeed premature.

There is considerable concern that many of the largest firms are not innovative. They are not generating efficient and effective new technology. They are not even generating competitive products on a world scale. The biggest companies in steel, autos, nonferrous metals, farm equipment, and consumer electronics have lost competitive battle after competitive battle. The financial guru's have noted the small firm effect, the economists have noted the innovation gap, and the entrepreneurs have noticed opportunity.

Entrepreneurship and Chauvinism

The deep recession of 1982–1983 focused considerable attention on the economic weakness of some of the largest firms. Many analysts focused hard on the innovative entrepreneur as the solution to the U.S. competitive disadvantage. Numerous studies have shown the association between entrepreneurship and innovation. The studies cited use both case examples and statistics to make their points. The National Science Foundation found that small companies produce four times more innovation per research dollar than bigger companies. Others examining the same study quote a figure of twenty-four times the number of innovations per dollar of research. Still others find that smaller firms are 2.5 times as innovative per employee as larger firms.

No matter which set of statistics is chosen, there is clear agreement among scholars and practitioners alike that smaller firms follow the economic logic of Schumpeter in his seminal work *The Views of Economic Development:* "You do not ask the owner of the stage line to build a railroad." The smaller firms do not face the constraints imposed by large investment in existing technology; thus they are both free and compelled to innovate. This is not to say that large firms are not critical to development, to cost-based efficiency, and to dealing with truly world-scale production processes. Nevertheless it is clear that smaller firms developed many important inventions, including xerography, air conditioning, the Polaroid process, cellophane, insulin, penicillin, helicopters, and ballpoint pens.

Smaller firms have the capability and the necessity to innovate. Although many opportunities eventually are pursued successfully by larger firms, it appears to be the smaller firms that attempt and succeed in leapfrogging existing technology.

The smaller, publicly traded firms with thinner capitalization seem to have done better than their larger competitors. In the steel industry, public firms with under $60 million in capitalization averaged 2.5 times better returns on equity than their larger counterparts in the same industry and even exceeded the returns of the larger computer firms over an eighteen-year period.

Thus innovation and profitability allow for competitiveness. The competitiveness was recognized by liberal and conservative alike as one of the potential keys to continuing U.S. competitiveness and thus to continued high standards of living for U.S. citizens.

Ideological Support for Entrepreneurship

There is a unique compatibility between the concept of entrepreneurship and the historically valued, rugged individualist. The Lockean support for individual sovereignty is played out in the economic field in the entrepreneurial arena. There is a vital nexus between the historic conservative interest in free enterprise in its most extreme form and the rebellious liberal ideology of the sixties. Much media and academic focus has been placed on this curious admixture of values. No statistical studies have shown high correlation, but the case-based data is clear. Many of those who were at the forefront of the 1960s' rebellion have found comfort in the independence of the entrepreneurial life. The media has delighted in the pictures of the bearded developers of the microcomputer Steven Jobs and Steven Wozniak. Many Silicon Valley entrepreneurs recount the significance of the sixties to the formation of their approaches to business, competition, and human resource management.

Other groups have prospered in the new entrepreneurial wave. The new immigrants from Asia have prospered and created great opportunity for themselves, their families, and the workforce. The Cuban migration to southern Florida has also spawned extensive entrepreneurial energy. Many of these individuals cite the link between the political and economic freedom as critical to their willingness and capability to seize the opportunities inherent in U.S. markets.

Psychological and Personal Rewards of Entrepreneurship

Early studies of entrepreneurship such as that of Collins, Moore, and Unwalla identified the entrepreneur as an outcast who was largely dissatisfied. Recent work must cast doubt on the generality of that conclusion. Certainly, there are questions regarding the methodology of

Table 1–4
Job Satisfies Personal Values
(percent)

	Self-Employed	*Work for Others*
To a great extent	53.6	34.6
To a significant extent	33.3	42.2
To some extent	9.4	15.4
Not significantly	3.6	7.8

Source: Howard H. Stevenson, *Who Are the Harvard Self-Employed?* Harvard University Graduate School of Business Administration Working Paper 9-783-042, 1983, 9.

that early study. When, for example, managers are compared with self-employed individuals with age and education held constant, the results are very different.

Paula Duffy and Howard H. Stevenson recently studied over six thousand graduates of Harvard University's Graduate School of Business Administration. Among the questions addressed were the degree to which their job satisfied their personal values, the nature of those values, and the degree to which they had achieved financial success. In each of these measures the entrepreneurially self-employed stood out as being significantly more rewarded by their careers than their classmates who had pursued administrative careers working for others.

The degree to which the self-employed found greater satisfaction in their jobs was striking. Table 1–4 shows this comparison. These values were somewhat different as shown in table 1–5.

Perhaps one of the greatest distinctions was the degree to which those who were self-employed had achieved financial success. The distinction between the two groups with similar training and background was remarkable (see table 1–6).

One can certainly not assert the generality of the findings taken from such a unique sample base, although the evidence from the *Forbes 400* survey would indicate that the road to wealth is either inheritance or self-employment.

Thus these data strongly reinforce any tendencies an individual might have to attempt to become an entrepreneur. The rewards are there both in terms of money and personal recognition. The environ-

Table 1–5
Four Most Important Job Values
(percentages)

	Self-Employed	Not Self-Employed
Economic	39.2	31.6
Other job features	29.9	40.2
External rewards	10.8	11.6
Life-style values	19.9	16.5

Source: Howard H. Stevenson, *Who Are the Harvard Self-Employed?* Harvard University Graduate School of Business Administration Working Paper 9-783-042, 1983, 23.

ment is conducive to acquiring control over resources that may be required to succeed. The sole problem may well be that the alternatives for the successful remain good, thereby inhibiting desire to pursue new opportunity.

Examining the concept of *entrepreneurship* yields much evidence of its importance. Further study is required to clarify the phenomena. This chapter has already used several terms: *self-employment, small business, founder.* Before proceeding further it will be useful to examine the definitions of these terms and others to determine their utility for analysis and ultimately for action.

Defining Entrepreneurship

Entrepreneurship was compared by Kilby to the Heffalump, that is, "it is a large and important animal which has been hunted by many individuals using various ingenious trapping devices. . . . All who claim to have caught sight of him report that he is enormous, but they disagree on his particularities. Not having explored his current habitat with sufficient care, some hunters have used as bait their own favorite dishes and have then tried to persuade people that what they caught was a Heffalump. However, very few are convinced, and the search goes on."

At the risk of adding to the confusion, it may be helpful to review the historic definitions applied and then to examine some descriptive behavioral characteristics that distinguish entrepreneurial behavior.

Table 1–6
Financial Net Worth Fifteen or More Years Following Graduation
(percentages)

	<$50,000	$50,000–$249,999	$250,000–$499,999	$500,000–$999,999	$1,000,000–$2,499,999	$2,500,000
Self-employed	11.0	11.2	17.7	14.6	29.2	24.8
Not self-employed	1.9	20.1	24.3	22.8	19.1	11.8

Source: Howard H. Stevenson, *Who Are the Harvard Self-Employed?* Harvard University Graduate School of Business Administration Working Paper 9-783-042, 1983, 48.

There are several schools of thought regarding entrepreneurship. These schools may be roughly divided into those who identify entrepreneurship with an economic function, those who identify it with an individual, and those who, like me, view it in behavioral terms.

The economic functional analysis of entrepreneurship focuses on the economic role rather than the individual who performs such a role. This emphasis on economic role was the historical wellspring of interest.

Richard Cantillon saw the economic function as bearing the risk of buying at certain prices and selling at future uncertain prices. This risk-bearing function was the definition coined by Cantillon when he first used the word *entrepreneurship* in the early eighteenth Century.[10] Jean Baptiste Say broadened the definition to include the concept of bringing together the factors of production.[11] This definition led others to question whether there was a unique entrepreneurial function or whether it was simply a form of management.

Schumpeter's work in 1911 added the concept of innovation to the notion of entrepreneurship. He allowed for many kinds of innovation including process innovation, market innovation, product innovation, factor innovation, and even organizational innovation. His seminal work emphasized the role of the entrepreneur in creating and responding to economic discontinuities. Although his work on business cycles assumed equilibrium as the normal state, he recognized that the fundamental source of disequilibrium was the entrepreneur.[12] Other participants in the Schumpeter coterie, Cole in particular, saw the entrepreneurial function as the primary administrator in the economic engine.[13]

It is clear that some of the more current popular definitions do not contribute very much to our understanding of entrepreneurship. Among the terms that have often been applied are *founder, creator,* and *risk taker.* Each of these terms focuses on some aspect of some entrepreneurs. But, if one has to be the *founder* to be an *entrepreneur,* then neither Thomas Watson of IBM nor Ray Kroc of McDonalds will qualify, making many people much less interested in the concept if it excludes such important examples of the kind of behavior in which they are interested. Although risk taking is an important element of entrepreneurial behavior, it is clear that many entrepreneurs bear risk grudgingly and only after they have made valiant attempts to get the capital sources and resource providers to bear the risk. As one extremely successful entrepreneur said, "My idea of risk and reward is for me to get the reward and others to take the risks." Creativity is clearly not a prerequisite for entrepreneurship. Many successful entrepreneurs have been good at copying others. They qualify as innovators and creators only by stretching the definition beyond elastic limits.

Identification of entrepreneurship with distinct individuals has spawned much research on the personal characteristics of entrepreneurs. Considerable effort has gone into the development of an understanding of the psychological and sociological wellsprings of entrepreneurship—as Kent refers to it, "supply-side entrepreneurship." These studies have noted some common modalities among entrepreneurs with respect to need for achievement, perceived locus of control, orientation toward intuitive rather than sensate thinking, and risk-taking propensity. In addition, many have commented on the common, but not universal, thread of childhood deprivation, minority group membership, and early adolescent economic experiences as typifying the entrepreneur. Pioneering work of Collins and Moore, McClelland, and the later work of Silver and Kao have made attempts to evaluate the psychosociological origins of the phenomenon. Some have systematically attempted comparative studies where the entrepreneurs are paired with similarly successful managers. Others have compared successful with unsuccessful entrepreneurs. Still others have not attempted controlled comparison but have simply identified the common characteristics. Implications in some of these studies as to causality are strong even though the methodologies in general can only show association.

Other critics of the supply-side school of entrepreneurship raise the traditional academic questions as to whether the psychological and social traits are either necessary or sufficient for the development of entrepreneurship. These traits are at best modalities and not universalities since many successful and unsuccessful entrepreneurs do not share the characteristics identified. Further, historical studies do not show the same character traits in earlier entrepreneurs. Also the studies of the life paths of entrepreneurs often show decreasing entrepreneurship following success. Such evidence at least raises a question whether the nature of entrepreneurship is immutably imbedded in the personality from early stages of childhood development.

Entrepreneurship as a Behavioral Phenomenon

In managerial terms, it does not appear useful to delimit the entrepreneur by defining those functions that are entrepreneurial and those that are not. Nor does it appear particularly helpful to decide which individuals are entrepreneurs and which are not. The first exercise appears to be rather more semantic than practical. The second appears to be fruitless in that individuals in our society may attempt entrepreneurship and often succeed even if they do not fit the standards of academic judges as to their entrepreneurial personality or sociological background.

The behavioral school would argue that certain outcomes are desirable for individuals, for organizations, and for society. Defining entrepreneurship in terms of these outcomes can help to provide mechanisms for inducing the desired behavior.

Experience shows that entrepreneurship as an economic function is not a single point but rather a range of behavior. There are six critical dimensions that distinguish entrepreneurial behavior from more administratively oriented behavior: (1) strategic orientation; (2) commitment to opportunity; (3) the resource commitment process; (4) the concept of control over resources; (5) the concept of management; and (6) compensation policy. I discard the notion that entrepreneurship is an all-or-none trait and examine the behavioral dimensions in terms of a range of behavior between extremes. At one extreme is the *promoter* type of manager who feels confident of his or her ability to seize opportunity regardless of the resources under current control. At the opposite extreme is the *trustee* type of manager who fosters efficient management by emphasizing the effective utilization of existing resources. There is an important role for both in our economy, but the entrepreneur who falls close to the promoter side of the spectrum may be uniquely suited to pursue opportunity today.

The Nature of Opportunity

Opportunity is the key element of entrepreneurship. Opportunity for this purpose has several important elements. First, it is a relativistic concept, that is, opportunities for individuals vary depending on age, previous accomplishments and financial resources, and even the social

Desired future state
involves growth or change

		Yes	No
		Entrepreneur	Satisfied manager
Self-perceived power to achieve goals	Yes	Entrepreneur	Satisfied manager
	No	Frustrated potential entrepreneur	Bureaucratic functionary

Figure 1–1. Manager's Opportunity Matrix

milieu in which the individual is functioning. Perhaps the reason that many studies have found entrepreneurship to arise frequently among the disadvantaged or among certain minorities has been that they have been systematically excluded from the personal opportunities that lie in traditional hierarchies either from a lack of the proper background or from outright prejudice. The reason some individuals become entrepreneurial after adversity is that their previous stream of opportunities had played out or become blocked. The reason that individuals become less entrepreneurial following success may well be that they have defined their personal opportunities along nonbusiness dimensions of power, prestige, and leisure or that they simply begin to focus on preservation of their existing resource base.

The implications of this concept of opportunity are clear. A possible situation becomes an opportunity when the results of the action are deemed desirable and feasible. A matrix defining entrepreneurship is shown in figure 1–1. One can see how the present position influences whether one is entrepreneurial or not. It is also clear that particular skills, talents, and attitudes toward risk influence the perception as to whether an outcome is feasible. Training, knowledge, and self-confidence contribute to such perceptions.

The importance of this figure cannot be overemphasized since individuals place themselves in their particular box for rational reasons relating to their own lives; however, for the firms desiring to build the entrepreneurial spirit, action is required.

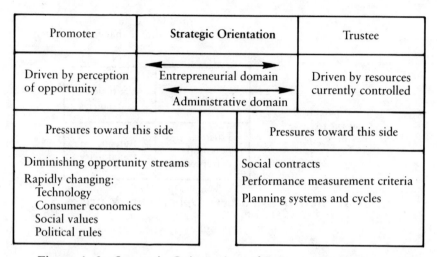

Promoter	Strategic Orientation		Trustee
Driven by perception of opportunity	Entrepreneurial domain ↔	↔ Administrative domain	Driven by resources currently controlled
Pressures toward this side		Pressures toward this side	

Diminishing opportunity streams
Rapidly changing:
  Technology
  Consumer economics
  Social values
  Political rules
		Social contracts
		Performance measurement criteria
		Planning systems and cycles	

Figure 1–2. Strategic Orientation of Promoter and Trustee

Promoter	Commitment to Opportunity		Trustee
Revolutionary with short duration	Entrepreneurial domain ↔	↔ Administrative domain	Evolutionary, of long duration, controlled
Pressures toward this side		Pressures toward this side	
Action orientation Short decision windows Risk management Limited decision constituencies		Acknowledgment of multiple constituencies Negotiation of strategy Risk reduction Management of fit	

Figure 1–3. Commitment to Opportunity of Promoter and Trustee

Strategic Orientation. The entrepreneur–promoter is oriented to opportunity whereas the administrator–trustee builds a strategy to use the resources currently controlled. Figure 1–2 shows this orientation and the pressures that drive the managers to the particular orientation. As can be seen, much of the force to the trusteeship orientation arises out of organization demands. The opportunity focus is a function of the changing environment.

Commitment to Opportunity. Where the promoter is committed to action, the doubt resides about the durability of the commitment. The trustee is slow to act, but the commitment is durable. There are obvious advantages in coping with a rapidly changing environment when the commitment can be made quickly and dropped just as quickly. Unfortunately, these factors are negative for the preservation of an organization as shown in figure 1–3.

Commitment of Resources. The entrepreneur–promoter is known for doing more with less. Many entrepreneurs start the pursuit of an opportunity with no resources other than the confidence that they have identified a real opportunity. The administrator–trustee's major preoccupation and source of personal reward is the effective administration of the resources currently controlled. The result is a very different process by which resources get committed to the pursuit of an identified opportunity. For the entrepreneur it is, perforce, multistaged as they are acquired from others. The entrepreneur is thus perceived as a gambler and tentative. The trustee often is simply responding to the source of the rewards offered (see figure 1–4).

Control of Resources. The entrepreneur–promoter is often horrified by overhead and the encumbrances that resources used in the business imply. The administrator–trustee is often compensated on the basis of the amount of assets under his or her management and the number of people employed. These are totally different attitudes and are responsive to very different measurement schemes. Figure 1–5 illustrates this difference.

Concepts of Management Structure. The orientation toward opportunity often brings with it the desire of the entrepreneur–promoter to keep in touch with all the key players and to be able to personally sell

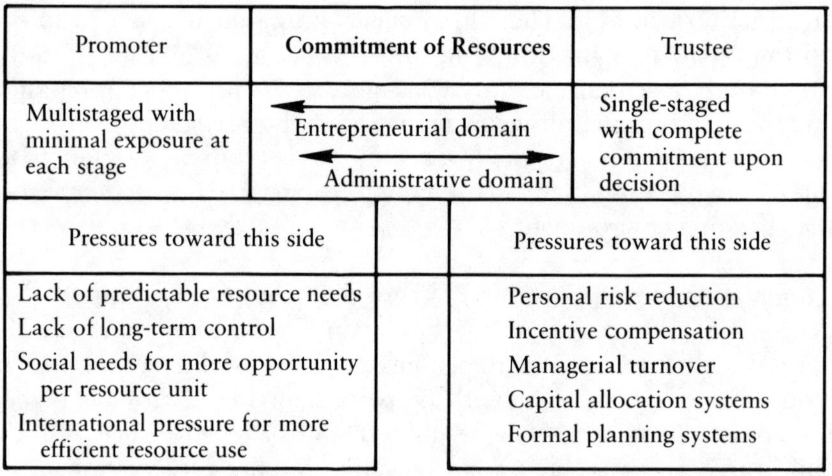

Promoter	**Commitment of Resources**	Trustee
Multistaged with minimal exposure at each stage	Entrepreneurial domain ⟷ ⟷ Administrative domain	Single-staged with complete commitment upon decision
Pressures toward this side		Pressures toward this side
Lack of predictable resource needs Lack of long-term control Social needs for more opportunity per resource unit International pressure for more efficient resource use		Personal risk reduction Incentive compensation Managerial turnover Capital allocation systems Formal planning systems

Figure 1–4. Commitment of Resources by Promoter and Trustee

Promoter	**Control of Resources**	Trustee
Episodic use of rent of required resources	Entrepreneurial domain ⟷ ⟷ Administrative domain	Ownership or employment of required resources
Pressures toward this side		Pressures toward this side
Increased resource specialization Long resource life compared to need Risk of obsolescence Risk inherent in any new venture Inflexibility of permanent commitment to resources		Power, status and financial rewards Coordination Efficiency measures Inertia and cost of change Industry structures

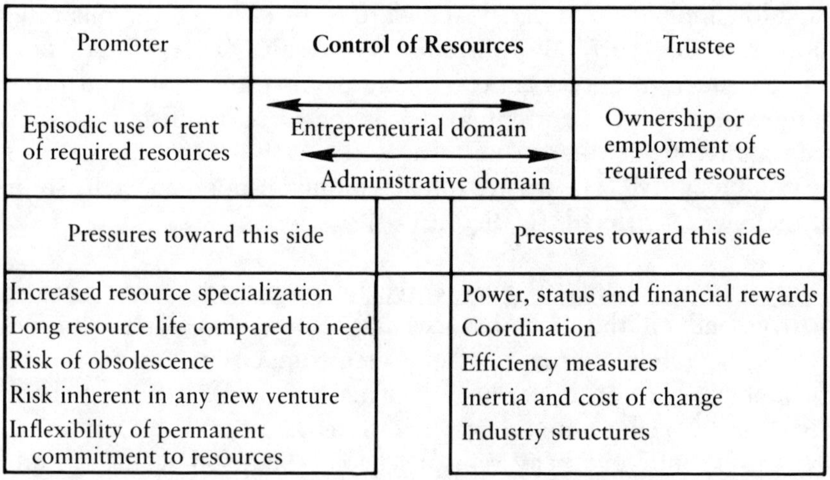

Figure 1–5. Control of Resources by Promoter and Trustee

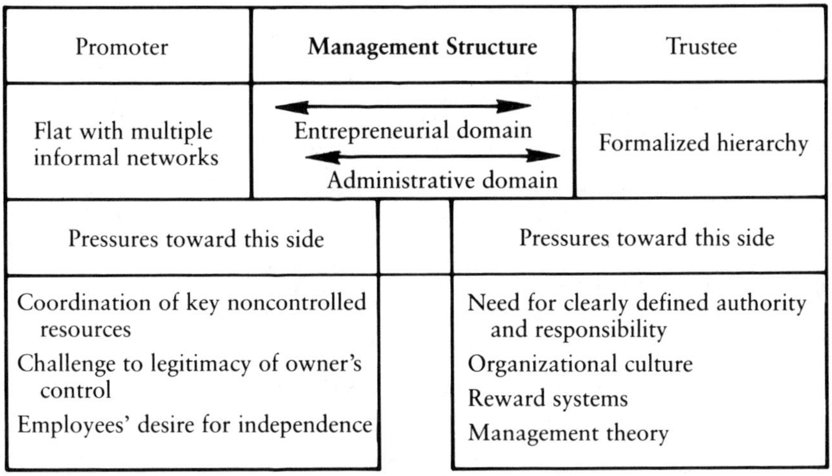

Promoter	**Management Structure**	Trustee
Flat with multiple informal networks	← Entrepreneurial domain → ← Administrative domain →	Formalized hierarchy
Pressures toward this side		Pressures toward this side
Coordination of key noncontrolled resources Challenge to legitimacy of owner's control Employees' desire for independence		Need for clearly defined authority and responsibility Organizational culture Reward systems Management theory

Figure 1–6. Management Structure of Promoter and Trustee

the concepts and involvement and to provide personal payoffs. The administrator–trustee often views organizations more formally, where responsibilities and authority should be well defined. The decision to use and to rent resources implies the necessity to manage in a different way. Figure 1–6 illustrates this distinction in management form.

Compensation–Reward Systems. Entrepreneurial organizations base compensation on value creation and on team performance, whereas administrative organizations base compensation on individual responsibility levels (for example, assets or resources under control) and on performance relative to short-term accounting targets (for example, profits or return on assets) and rely heavily on promotion as a means of reward. Figure 1–7 shows these differences and lists some of the factors underlying each solution to the issue of how to measure and reward employees.

There is no intended implication that entrepreneurship is important and trusteeship is not. In fact, the goal of entrepreneurship is often the creation of value and wealth. Success in the pursuit of the entrepreneurial goal thus leads ever more strongly to the need for effective trusteeship.

In developing the behavioral theory of entrepreneurship. It becomes clear that entrepreneurship is more than the individual or the

Promoter	Compensation–Reward Policy		Trustee⁄
Value-based, team-based, unlimited	← Entrepreneurial domain → ← Administrative domain →		Resource-based, driven by short-term data, promotion, limited amount
Pressures toward this side		Pressures toward this side	
Individual expectations Competition Increased perception of personal wealth creation possibilities		Societal norms IRS regulations Impacted information Search for simple solutions to complex problems Demands of public shareholders	

Figure 1–7. Compensation and Reward Policies of Promoter and Trustee

economic function. It is a cohesive pattern of consistent behavior that is vital to individuals, to organizations, and to societies in changing times. As old opportunities yield less value to those who exploit them, new ones must be pursued. Unfortunately, much that is done to manage the fruits of previous success reduces the possibility of effectively pursuing new success.

Summary

If entrepreneurship is important, then organizations and society must find ways to encourage it. The data presented argue strongly that it is important and it is in fact different from simple good business practice as previously defined. The individual entrepreneur is a person who perceives opportunity, finds the pursuit of opportunity desirable in the context of his or her life situation, and believes that success is possible. These elements distinguish the entrepreneur from the vast majority of people. In the individual, these three aspects have certain manifestations. The individual's ability to perceive opportunity is founded on knowledge of products and markets. The entrepreneur has to have a better idea for a product or service and/or a better way to deliver that product or service to a paying customer. The desire to pursue opportunity is based on a complex balancing of risk and reward. Success often is the major impediment to continual pursuit of healthy change. It is fortunate that success is perceived as valuable and failure is seen as only temporary or else few would try. Individual entrepreneurs believe success is possible. Often this belief is founded on the example of the friends and associates with whom the start-up entrepreneur can identify. There must also be a belief and a commitment to the outcome. Delusions are costly if they are reflected in misperception of markets, technologies, or economics.

For individuals and for organizations these same three factors must be built into the organization life. The factors cannot be perpetuated by cloning founders or by developing a mechanistic set of rules that insure extensions of the brilliant thoughts of the leader. They require building an adaptive organization and society.

Entrepreneurship is critical. Change must be seen as desirable if we are to respond to the new economic and technological environment. Organizing to pursue opportunity is the theme of the decade for the individual and for our best organizations. Entrepreneurship is more than a word, it is a mission. We must perceive opportunities inherent in change, we must create a desire for pursuing the opportunities that arise, and we must create an environment in which success is possible and the consequences of failure are tolerable.

References

Birch, David. *The Job Generation Process*. Cambridge, Mass.: MIT Program on Neighborhood and Regional Change, 1979.

Cantillon, Richard. *Essai sur la Nature du Commerce en Général*. Paris: Institute national d'Etudes Démographic, 1955. Originally published in 1952.

Cole, Arthur H. *Business Enterprise in Its Social Setting*. Cambridge, Mass.: Harvard University Press, 1959.

Collins, Orvis, David G. Moore, and Darab V. Unwalla. *The Enterprising Man*. East Lansing, Mich.: Michigan State University Business Studies, 1964.

Forbes Magazine, October 28, 1985.

Kao, John. *Entrepreneurs and Managers: Are They Different?* Cambridge, Mass.: Harvard University Graduate School of Business, Working Paper Series, 1985.

Kent, Calvin A. "The Rediscovery of the Entrepreneur," in *The Environment for Entrepreneurship,* ed. Calvin A. Kent. Lexington, Mass.: Lexington Books, 1984.

Kilby, Peter. *Entrepreneurship and Economic Development.* New York: Free Press, 1971.

Say, Jean Baptiste. *Catechism of Political Economy: Or, Familiar Conversations on the Manner in Which Wealth is Produced, Distributed and Consumed by Society.* London: Sherwood, 1815.

Schumpeter, Joseph A. *The Theory of Economic Development.* Cambridge, Mass.: Harvard University Press, 1934. First published in German in 1911.

Science Indicators. Washington, D.C.: National Science Foundation, 1979.

Silver, David A. *The Entrepreneurial Life: How to Go for It and Get it.* New York: John Wiley and Sons, 1982.

The State of Small Business: A Report of the President. Washington, D.C.: Government Printing Office, 1985.

2

Role of Entrepreneurship in Economic Development

Donald L. Sexton

S tudies conducted by David Birch and his associates in 1979 implied that the small business sector in the United States had saved the nation from economic stagnation or depression during the 1960s and early 1970s and that this sector would provide the impetus to economic growth and expansion in the future. Birch reported that 66 percent of all new jobs generated during the 1960s and early 1970s were in smaller firms that were less than five years old and had twenty or fewer employees.[1] Given that new business initiations average about 500,000 per year, then 66 percent of the new jobs were generated in about 2.5 million of the 12 million nonfarming smaller businesses in the United States during this period.

Subsequent studies by the Brookings Institution cast doubt on some of the results in the Birch study.[2] As a result, Birch in a later study concluded that a significant percentage of all new jobs were generated by only a relatively small percentage (12–15 percent) of the small business sector and that these firms were clustered in a few industries.[3] Thus, the findings of the original study attributing the bulk of the new jobs generated to the small business sector were modified to reflect that the new jobs were generated in a relatively small number of firms within the small business sector. Using the same rationale as before, one could assume that 12–15 percent of the 2.5 million firms, less than five years old, or 300,000–375,000 entrepreneurial growth-oriented firms generated the bulk of new jobs during the 1960s to early 1970s.

For the period 1976 to 1982, firms with twenty or fewer employees generated 38.5 percent of the total 11.8 million new jobs generated or a total of 4.6 million new jobs.[4] Assuming the same ratios as before, the majority of the 4.6 million new jobs were generated by roughly four hundred thousand growth-oriented firms. This growth orientation leads to innovation, job creation, and economic expansion. The growth orientation has also been attributed by many to be the difference between entrepreneurial firms and the multitude of other small firms that have little impact on economic development. Thus, it is the relatively few entrepreneurial firms within the small business sector and not the entire sector that has a significant impact on the economic development of a region, state, or country. Consequently, initiatives to attract or initiate firms that will contribute to economic development should be directed toward entrepreneurial growth-oriented firms and not toward small businesses in general.

A significant factor about growth or growth orientation is that it is not inevitable, nor does it occur of and by itself. It is a conscious decision made by some business owners and avoided by others. However, the importance of growth–no growth decisions on the economic development of an area are of such importance that a review of the literature related to this phenomenon and to the entrepreneurs that made these decisions appears warranted.

Growth Theory

Initially growth theory was introduced as an aspect of economic development by Schumpeter.[5] A general theory of growth was presented in 1953 by Boulding.[6] Levy noted that growth "is a systematic process of development; . . . is purposeful; . . . does not progress uniformly; . . . is affected by and affects the environment; [involves] personal leadership of top management; and the proclivity of management to take risk or to innovate."[7]

Dominant in growth literature is the metamorphosis stage model, which views growth not as a continuous process but one of discreet changes. The main theme is that a firm passes through a number of stages. Although there are differences in the number of stages suggested, the majority of authors delineate three or four. Filley's included three stages: "The Traditional (Craft) Company; Dynamic Growth; and Rational Administration."[8] The impetus for transition from stage 1 to stage 2 is disequilibrium caused by the introduction and promotion of an innovation. It also requires an entrepreneur to guide it through the time of uncertainty. Although metamorphosis models abound (Davis,[9] Dale,[10] Drucker,[11] Kleppner,[12] Steinmetz,[13] Stanworth and Curran,[14] and Churchill and Lewis,[15]), some disagreement exists as to the applicability or appropriateness to smaller businesses.

Stanworth and Curran, in evaluating stage models, found fault in a number of areas: "These various approaches do contain a considerable element of truth but this derives at least partly from the definitional procedures used in theory construction."[16] They further objected on the basis that:

1. The implied characteristics of the firm's organizational and managerial structure contained within the latter stages in most of the models strongly indicates that the authors are discussing a firm which has long since entered the 6 percent of larger firms in our economy, . . .

2. The theories of small firm growth, constructed upon the positivest view, fail to meet their self-imposed standards.

3. The assumption that natural and social phenomena belong to the same category of entities for purposes of theorizing and explanation is fundamentally mistaken. The crucial difference stems from the fact that social phenomena understand their own behavior and can act purposefully while natural phenomena have neither of these properties.[17]

The last point made by Stanworth and Curran indicates that growth problems or opportunities, as stated earlier, are under the control of the entrepreneur. He or she can initiate the growth, foster it, nurture it, and prune it as desired.

Churchill and Lewis found similar problems with growth theories.

Each uses business size as one dimension and company maturity or the stage of growth as a second dimension. While useful in many respects, these frameworks are inappropriate for small business on at least three counts. First, they assume that a company must grow and pass through all stages of development or die in the attempt. Second, the models fail to capture the important early stages in a company's origin and growth. Third, these frameworks characterize company size largely in terms of annual sales and ignore other factors such as value added, number of locations, complexity of product line, and rate of change in product or production technology.[18]

Organizational life cycle theory may be questioned due to underlying concepts that are suspect. Perhaps the theory cannot be accurately applied. Further, there seems to be no consistent element of time. Some firms never grow, whereas others experience such rapid growth that they seem to pass over some defined stages. Some firms remain in the early stages for years and never achieve the growth of newer organizations. Further, maturity or decline, as a final stage, may be prolonged or avoided through product innovation, geographic expansion, or other initiatives.

In summary, although there are general patterns for growth, there seems to be no simple pattern of growth. As Levy notes, structural growth (which includes organizations) "is much more difficult to reduce to a neat set of propositions."[19]

The Growth or No-Growth Decision

As noted earlier, growth is a controllable factor. If an organization must grow to survive, then why do not all businesses either grow or die? With about 12 million nonfarming small businesses in the United States, is it a valid assumption that in a few years there will be 12 million large businesses? If metamorphosis models apply, may one assume all will grow and eventually die? More likely, a few will grow, many will survive at or close to existence levels, and others will die. Might the determining factor be a conscious decision to grow or not to grow? If so, it is the individual's determination.

In developing a typology of entrepreneurs and their motivations toward growth, Stanworth and Curran defined three "identities" of entrepreneurs; the artisan role, the classical role, and the manager role.[20] The *artisan* entrepreneur's role centers around intrinsic or personal satisfaction. This entrepreneur is very concerned with intrinsic satisfactions likely to minimize psychological deprivations of social marginality. The *classical* entrepreneur is defined as a person much more concerned with maximization of financial returns than with intrinsic satisfaction. As financial returns are maximized through growth, a new identity, that of *manager,* emerges as the entrepreneur takes action to ensure the continued success of the firm. This action is exemplified in the delegation of management functions and the development of a more rational bureaucratic structure. The most problematic situation, according to Stanworth and Curran, is that where the owner–manager attempts to make the transition from an artisan to a classical entrepreneur identity.

Smith found that two different types of entrepreneurs could be isolated. He identified a *craftsman* entrepreneur as "characterized by narrowness in education and training, low social awareness and involvement, a feeling of incompetence in dealing with the social environment, and a limited time horizon."[21] Smith hypothesized that a craftsman entrepreneur does not have a growth orientation and that growth does not occur as the result of a craftsman entrepreneur changing his or her role. Rather, growth occurs from a different type of person or an *opportunistic* entrepreneur, described as "exhibiting breadth in education and training, high social awareness and involvement, confidence in his/her ability to deal with the social environment, and an awareness of, and orientation to the future."[22] Smith found that adaptive firms headed by opportunistic entrepreneurs experienced growth rates nearly nine times as great as firms headed by craftsman entrepreneurs. The implications of his findings were that for firms to develop from businesses to substantial corporations a basic change in style may not necessarily occur. Rather, firms grow as a result of a different type of entrepreneur, that is, an opportunistic entrepreneur, directing the firm.

Smith and Miner applied role-motivation theory in an attempt to further develop Smith's earlier work related to craftsman and opportunistic types of entrepreneurs.[23] They found that the average level of role-motivation for both types of entrepreneurs was relatively low in comparison to that of managers in large bureaucratic organizations. This implies that, although entrepreneurs can support growth to larger firms, there is a limit to the amount of growth. Their findings also supported earlier studies indicating that the opportunistic entrepreneur is associated with a more adaptive (growth-oriented) pattern. However, they were unable to find support for the hypothesis that role motivation was the driving factor behind the opportunistic entrepreneur's growth orientation.

Carland et al. delineated between growth orientation (entrepreneur) and no growth orientation (small business owners) on the basis of personal and/or profit motives and on the present and/or future orientation (strategic management) of the owner. They describe a small business owner as "an individual who establishes and manages a business for the principal purpose of furthering personal goals. . . . The owner perceives the business as an extension of his or her personality, intricately bound with family needs and desires."[24]

Contrasted with the small business owner, the entrepreneur is defined as "an individual who establishes and manages a business for the principal purposes of profit and growth . . . characterized principally by innovative behavior and employs strategic management practices in the business."[25]

The differences between the definitions of Stanworth and Curran, Smith, and Carland et al. are mostly sematic. What Stanworth and Curran call an artisan entrepreneur, Smith describes as a craftsman entrepreneur, and Carland et al. call small business. Further, the difference between classical, opportunistic, and growth entrepreneur also are only sematic.

Thus, the decision to grow or not to grow lies with the owner–manager. If the owner–manager is more than a self-employed person or a person filling an income substitution or wage alternative position and desires to participate in growth for the firm, the growth becomes the entrepreneurial event that leads to innovation, job creation, and economic expansion. This is entrepreneurship.

The impact of job generation and its subsequent impact on economic development as related in the Birch studies and others shows that the bulk of the growth in the small business sector is the result of a relatively small number of growth-oriented firms. Theories related to growth of firms and the decision to grow or not to grow have been reviewed, and a hypothesis that entrepreneurship includes the element of growth that leads to innovation, job creation, and economic expansion, has been developed. Not all growth is limited to very small firms. There are other growth-oriented firms that, because of their growth orientation, have outgrown the term *small*. An analysis of their growth is provided by reviewing the impact of the *INC.*'s 500 fastest growing private companies and 100 fastest growing small public companies on the economic development of the United States.

INC. 500 Fastest-Growing Private Companies

The *INC.* 500 lists the fastest-growing privately held companies in the United States, ranked by percentage increase in sales from fiscal year

1979 through fiscal year 1983.[26] The criteria for being considered for the *INC.* 500 are that they must (1) be privately held; (2) have been in business for a minimum of five years; (3) have annual sales between $100,000 and $25 million; and (4) have a sales increase in 1983 over 1982. *INC.* estimated that more than five hundred thousand firms met the criteria for consideration. Their list includes only the fastest-growing 500 privately held companies.

For the 500 companies, total sales in 1983 were roughly $5.7 billion compared to $522 million in 1979, an increase of 992 percent. The 500 companies averaged $1 million in sales in 1979. By 1983, the firms averaged more than $11 million in sales. The impact on total employment within the 500 firms was also quite dramatic. The total number of employees for the 500 firms in 1983 was 58,605 compared to 11,668 in 1979, a 402 percent increase. The average number of employees per firm increased from 23 in 1979 to 117 in 1983.

The economic development of several states has benefitted from the growth of these entrepreneurial firms: California is home to 86 of the companies, Texas hosts 38, with 32 in Virginia, 31 in New York, and 26 in both Florida and Ohio.

The impact on the economic development of the United States of the *INC.* 500 fastest-growing privately held firms has been substantial. It is even more significant when one considers that these are only the 500 fastest-growing firms from a list, estimated by *INC.* to be greater than five hundred thousand.

Many of the *INC.* 500 firms have, by virtue of their growth, outgrown the small business sector. Further, there are additional firms that are also expanding rapidly. The *INC.* 100 list of the fastest-growing small public companies describes the impact of firms slightly larger than the privately held firms.

INC. 100 Fastest-Growing Small Public Companies

The criteria for selection of the *INC.* 100 fastest-growing small public companies is different from the *INC.* 500 privately held companies in only two aspects: (1) the firms must have been publicly held as of December 31, 1983; and (2) they must have achieved a growth rate of at least 400 percent over the last five years. *INC.* estimates that these 100 firms are the fastest growing of roughly thirteen thousand firms that meet the criteria for consideration.[27]

The combined sales for the 100 fastest-growing small public companies for 1983 was $4.457 billion, up from $221 million in 1979, a 2000 percent increase in five years. It is interesting to note that the average sales of the 100 firms in 1983 was $44.6 million, yet only four of these 100 firms had sales in excess of $10 million in 1979. Growth in employment, although not as dramatic as sales growth, was nonetheless quite significant. In 1979 the 100 firms employed 5,410 persons. By 1983, the number of employees had grown to 50,578, an 834 percent increase.

As indicated earlier, growth is not inevitable, nor does it occur of and by itself. It is a conscious decision that when successfully implemented results in innovation, job creation, and economic development.

Factors Affecting New Venture Initiation and Growth

The economic impact of only a relatively small number of firms has been significant. Areas desiring to encourage economic development through assisting in the development of new business ventures have recognized that fledgling firms need assistance. Consequently, a number of new business incubator units have been funded by federal, state, and local governments, universities, private individuals and foundations, and corporations to provide assistance to the new business. The general goals of the incubators are to create jobs through the development of new business firms and to stimulate entrepreneurship. The incubator is a relatively new and rapid-growing concept that provides the new firm with access to low-cost facilities and services. As the firms develop and prosper, they graduate from the incubator to being completely self-sufficient. According to a survey by Smilor, roughly 90 percent of the incubators have been in existence less than three years.[28]

The new business incubator should not be confused with an incubator organization. Incubator organizations are those firms that appear to have a propensity for employing and training individuals who

later establish their own new ventures. These newly established ventures emanating from larger corporations are often referred to as *spin-off* companies. Although not confined to a particular industry, they do appear to be more frequent and are more successful in the high-technology industry sector.

Perhaps the most famous incubator organization is Fairchild Semiconductors, which spawned a total of thirty seven spin-offs from 1957 to 1970.[29]

Both the business incubator and the incubator organization will ultimately affect the location of the new business venture. It is anticipated that the business incubator will become the incubator organization but for different reasons. The purpose of the business incubator is to create *graduates* or *spin-offs*. The incubator organization basically loses an employee or a group of employees when they leave to start their own business. Studies by Cooper of new technology business spin-offs in the San Francisco area during the period 1960–1969 showed that 85 percent of the new businesses located close to the incubator organization and that the spin-offs from smaller firms occurred at a much higher rate than from larger ones.[30] The reasons supporting the location proximity appear to result from a desire to continue established networks with suppliers, resources, and others and an unwillingness to disrupt the lives of the family by moving to another location. The support rationale for the spin-offs from smaller firms stems from the experience and familiarity of a smaller firm being more directly applicable than that of a larger firm in the development of the new venture.[31]

Jennings and Sexton argue that if larger firms were to develop a corporate climate that encouraged innovation, creativity, and entrepreneurship, the number of spin-offs would be drastically reduced.[32] Cooper further suggests that new high-technology firms are desirable for economic development because they offer possibilities for great growth, produce little noise or pollution, account for a disproportionately high share of major technological innovations, have a relatively high success rate, and add vitality and flexibility to the economy.[33]

For the most part, the impact of controllable local environmental factors on the decision to initiate a new venture is limited to three factors: (1) demonstration effects; (2) financial support; and (3) a supportive environment. According to the new venture initiation model developed by Martin, these are only three of the nine factors that affect the new venture start-up. Paraphrasing Martin, there is a substantial chance that an individual will launch a new venture if the individual's readiness to act (psychological make-up, social background, and the experience of a demonstrative model in a parent and/or colleague/ mentor in an incubator organization) is present in conjunction with an experience of a precipitating event (job dissatisfaction, dismissal, or layoff) in a period of unencumbered financial/family problems, and in a supportive environment which includes family, financial, and other services.[34]

Impact of Local Initiatives on New Venture Creation

A city, state, or other area desiring to enhance economic development through local initiatives can have an impact on only three of the nine factors considered necessary in new venture start-up. However, these three factors—demonstration effects, financial support, and supportive environment—are of major importance in the new venture decision process.

Demonstration effects are those actions or examples of others that lead the potential entrepreneur to feel that he or she has the capability not only to create a new venture but to develop it into a successful business. The incubator organization is one important aspect of a demonstration effect. If an area lacks the existing larger businesses, a new business incubator can be developed through local, state, or private funding to generate the same effect.

Within the financial support area, an understanding of the problems of new businesses among the financial institutions and a desire to assist in their financial needs will provide a strong impetus to the development of new business ventures. These are especially effective when combined with local tax and utility incentives as well as the services provided by the new business incubator.

Finally, a supportive environment with a "can do" attitude among the educational services and the professional consultants combined with assistance in training, transportation, and state and local advisory services all seem to contribute to what has been described by many as an entrepreneurial climate.

Summary

Entrepreneurship plays an important role in the economic development of an area. Entrepreneurial firms are those growth-oriented firms that exist not only in the small business sector but also among the privately held and smaller public corporations that have outgrown the small business label.

Growth is a conscious, controllable factor that does not occur in and of itself. It must be planned and coordinated. It is not limited to a single industry or business but does appear to have a higher probability of success in the high-technology area.

Incubator organizations or new business incubator units have a major impact on the economic development of an area since the spin-offs or graduates tend to remain in the local community and enjoy higher probabilities of success.

A number of factors affect the decision to initiate a new venture. Some of these factors can be developed or encouraged through local initiatives. An area desiring to have an impact on its economic development would be well advised to develop the initiatives that foster the decision to initiate a new venture and to nurture the new organization during its early stages.

Notes

1. David L. Birch, *The Job Generation Process* (Cambridge, Mass.: MIT Program for Neighborhood and Regional Change, 1979).

2. Katherine Armington and Marjorie Odle, "Small Business: How Many Jobs," *Brookings Review* (Winter 1982).

3. David L. Birch and Susan McCracken, *The Small Business Share of Job Creation, Lessons Learned from the Use of Longitudinal File* (Washington, D.C.: Small Business Administration, 1982).

4. *The State of Small Business: A Report of the President* (Washington, D. C.: Government Printing Office, 1985), 19.

5. Joseph A. Schumpeter, *The Theory of Economic Development* (Cambridge, Mass.: Harvard University Press, 1934).

6. Kenneth E. Boulding, "Towards a General Theory of Growth," *Canadian Journal of Economics and Political Science* 19 (1943): 326–340.

7. A. M. Levy, "Growth Characteristics Applied to the Business Enterprise" (Ph.D. diss., New York University, 1966), 18.

8. Alan C. Filley and Robert J. House, *Managerial Process and Organization Behavior* (Glenview, Ill.: Scott, Foresman, 1969), 440.

9. Ralph C. Davis, *The Fundamentals of Management* (New York: Harper and Brothers, 1951).

10. Ernest Dale, *Planning and Developing the Company Organization Structure* (New York: American Management Association, 1952).

11. Peter Drucker, *The Practice of Management* (New York: Harper and Brothers, 1954).

12. Otto Kleppner, *Advertising Procedure* (New York: Prentice-Hall, 1955).

13. Lawrence L. Steinmetz, "Critical Stages of Small Business Growth: When They Occur and How to Survive Them," *Business Horizons* 12 (1969): 29–36.

14. M. I. K. Stanworth and J. Curran, "Growth and the Small Firm—An Alternative View," *Journal of Management Studies* 13 (May 1976): 95–110.

15. Neil C. Churchill and Virginia L. Lewis, "The Five Stages of Small Business Growth," *Harvard Business Review* 61 (May–June 1983): 30–50.

16. Stanworth and Curran, "Growth of the Small Firm," 98.

17. Ibid., 98.

18. Neil C. Churchill and Virginia L. Lewis, "The Five Stages of Small Business Growth," 31.

19. Levy, "Growth Characteristics," 21.

20. Stanworth and Curran, "Growth of the Small Firm," 105.

21. Norman Smith, *The Entrepreneur and His Firm: The Relationship between Type of Man and Type of Company* (East Lansing, Mich.: Bureau of Business and Economic Research, Michigan State University, 1967), 30.

22. Ibid., 58.

23. Norman Smith and John Miner, "Type of Entrepreneur, Type of Firm and Managerial Motivation: Implications for Organizational Life Cycle Theory," *Strategic Management Journal* 4 (October–December 1983): 325–340.

24. James W. Carland, Francis Hoy, William Boulton, and Joanne A. Carland, "Differentiating Entrepreneurs and Small Business Owners: A Conceptualization," *Academy of Management Review* 9 (April 1984): 358.

25. Ibid., 358.

26. "Inside the INC. 500," *INC.* 6 (December 1984): 52–53.

27. "The INC. 100," *INC.* 6 (May 1984): 155–157.

28. Raymond W. Smilor, "The New Business Incubator in America" (paper delivered at the First International Technological Innovation and Entrepreneurship Symposium, Salt Lake City, September 1985).

29. Michael J. C. Martin, *Managing Technological Innovation and Entrepreneurship* (Reston, Va.: Reston Publishing Co., 1984), 257.

30. Arnold C. Cooper, "Contrasts in the Role of Incubator Organizations in the Founding of Growth Oriented Firms," in *Frontiers of Entrepreneurship Research,* ed. John A. Hornaday, Fred A. Tarpley, Jr., Jeffrey A. Timmons, and Karl H. Vesper (Wellesley: Mass.: Babson Center for Entrepreneurial Studies, 1984), 160.

31. Ibid., 162.

32. Daniel F. Jennings and Donald L. Sexton, "Managing Innovation in Established Firms and Its Impact on Economic Growth and Employment," in *Proceedings of the NSF/RPI Conference on Industrial Science and Technology,* ed. Pier Abetti, Christopher Le Maistre, and William A. Wallace (Rochester, N.Y.: Center for Research and Development, Rensselaer Polytechnic Institute, 1985), 185.

33. Arnold C. Cooper, "Entrepreneurship and High Technology," in *The Art and Science of Entrepreneurship,* ed. Donald L. Sexton and Raymond W. Smilor (Cambridge, Mass.: Ballinger, 1986), 153.

34. Michael J. C. Martin, *Managing Technological Innovation and Entrepreneurship,* 269.

Part II
Role of New-Company Creation in Economic Development

3
Building Indigenous Companies: The Technology Venturing Approach

Raymond W. Smilor

The United States is in the midst of a great entrepreneurial era. Cities and regions across the country are finding creative and innovative ways to build indigenous companies. These responses comprise a new approach to assisting the economic renaissance of an area, known as *technology venturing*.

Technology venturing is an entrepreneurial process by which individuals and institutions—universities; federal, state, and local governments; and private and nonprofit sectors—take and share risk in integrating and commercializing scientific research, new technologies, and business opportunities. Technology venturing often links public sector initiatives and private sector investments to spur economical growth and technological diversification. Eight interactive stimulants are generating the technology venturing process.[1]

Imaginative Collaborative Relationships between Universities and Corporations. Universities and corporations are building stronger and more extensive ties to commercialize science and technology. Appendix 3A shows selected university–corporation programs. It indicates the scope of business firms, the diversity of research activities, the substantial amounts of funding, and the range of academic institutions involved in developing collaborative ties. These programs seek to speed the technology transfer process. They also provide an important window on emerging technology opportunities for business development.

Pioneering Programs and Linkages between Government, Business, and Universities. The federal government has taken the lead in providing for new applied research and development programs. The National Science Foundation (NSF), for example, has initiated a landmark effort in supercomputers, whereas the National Aeronautics and Space Administration (NASA) is advancing space commercialization. NSF has established supercomputer research centers in four major universities—Princeton University, University of California at San Diego, Cornell University, and University of Illinois. NASA is in the process of establishing space commercialization centers at six other geographically dispersed universities. The centers maintain critical links with business and reflect a new role for the university in economic development.

Innovative Private Joint Efforts for Scientific Advances. The Cooperative Research Act, which was passed by the U.S. Congress in October 1984, sanctioned and encouraged private consortia for research and development. These consortia reflect both a recognition of the realities of a truly international marketplace and a realization of financial, scientific, and human requirements for advanced research and development. The Microelectronics and Computer Technology Corporation in Austin, Texas, is a consortium of twenty-one companies in the computer industry. The Semiconductor Research Corporation in Research Triangle Park, North Carolina, brings together thirty-three companies in the semiconductor industry. The Advanced Television Research Center in Boston, Massachusetts, includes each of the major television networks. These examples of R&D consortiums are remarkable because they signal new types of collaborative ventures among intensely competitive firms.

A Blossoming Venture Capital Industry. Venture capital is growing rapidly in the United States. Over $3 billion was committed to venture capital pools in 1984 and over $2 billion was disbursed to venture-backed companies. Two-thirds to three-fourths of these disbursements went to technology-based companies.[2]

Creative Institutional Arrangements between the Public, Private, and Nonprofit Sectors. Foundations are playing an increasingly important role in economic development. Through endowments to universities, support of consortium efforts, and involvement in research centers, they are finding ways to help diversify regional and state economies.

Imaginative Local Community Initiatives for Economic Growth and Social Development. Local governmental entities, chambers of commerce, and city research groups and task forces are pushing economic diversification. They are finding new ways to link efforts and build community consensus. The Project '90 effort in San Antonio, Texas, is a prime example of effective community initiatives and leadership. By pulling together business, government, academic, and community constituencies, Project '90 addressed key city issues, developed 177 action initiatives, and charted a new strategic direction for San Antonio.[3]

Leading-edge State Government Growth Initiatives Fostering High Technology. States governments are taking a leadership role in diversifying regional economies through technology diversification. They are initiating programs for high-technology development, technology education, vocational training, and technical assistance. They are establishing seed capital funds. They are also setting up task forces to address special issues and to respond to important business location and relocation projects.[4]

Selected Federal Government Programs. In a number of ways, the federal government is acting as a stimulant to new business development. One of the most successful programs has been the Small Business Innovation Research (SBIR) program. Twelve federal government agencies have been mandated by Congress to set aside a percentage of their budgets to award to small businesses for technology development. The program operates on a competitive and phased process. From 1983 to 1988, the period covered by the current legislation, it is estimated that the SBIR program will fund over $1 billion in new monies to small businesses for R&D work.

These stimulants are having a dramatic impact on the entrepreneurial process.

The Entrepreneurial Process

Economic development[5] is based on four critical factors:

1. Talent—people
2. Technology—ideas
3. Capital—resources
4. Know-how—knowledge

Entrepreneurial talent results from the drive, tenacity, dedication, and hard work of special individuals—people who make things happen. Entrepreneurs are individuals who recognize opportunities. Where there is a pool of such talented entrepreneurial people, there is the opportunity for growth, diversification, and new business development. There are a variety of sources for entrepreneurs: universities, corporations, research labs, communities, the public sector, and inventors of all sorts. Events that trigger their entrepreneurial push may include dissatisfaction with current employment, recognition of an opportunity, an urge to try a new venture, changes in public policy, or simply a desire to push an innovative idea.

Talent without ideas, though, is like seed without water. The second critical component in the entrepreneurial process concerns the ability to generate ideas that have real potential within a reasonable time. The burst of creativity and innovation in emerging technological industries holds tremendous promise for economic development and technology business growth. When talent is linked with technology, people recognize and then push viable ideas and the entrepreneurial process is underway.

Every dynamic process needs to be fueled. The fuel for the entrepreneurial process is capital, which is the catalyst in the entrepreneurial chain reaction. It is the lifeblood of emerging and expanding enterprises. It is the *sine qua non* in business of a new product, an innovative service, or a brilliant idea. It provides the financial resource through which the ideas of the entrepreneur can be realized.

Given talent, technology, and capital, one other element is indispensible to making the entrepreneurial process successful. Know-how is the ability to leverage business or scientific knowledge in linking talent, technology, and capital in emerging and expanding enterprises. It is the ability to find and apply expertise in a variety of areas that can make the difference between success and failure. This expertise may involve management, marketing, finance, accounting, production, and manufacturing as well as legal, scientific, and engineering help.

Hypercompetition

The business climate is fierce both domestically and internationally. The competition is between countries, states, and communities as well as between large and small firms and among industries. The environment in which yet-to-be-born, born, and emerging firms must operate is particularly unforgiving. The ability to introduce new technologies or services to the marketplace poses several unique competitive problems.

To help companies meet the challenge of a hypercompetitive environment and to maximize the contributions of the small business and technology business growth sectors to the U.S. economy, the promotion of new business growth has become an important facet of economic policy at the federal, state, and local levels. Building indigenous companies has become an essential element in regional economic development.

Industrial relocation, long the central focus of regional economic development, tends to be a zero-sum game—one region or location benefits only at the expense of another. Indigenous company growth may be a more beneficial and necessary long-term economic development strategy for several reasons. First, it harnesses local entrepreneurial talent. Second, it builds companies that in turn creates jobs and thus adds economic value to a region and community. Third, this strategy keeps home-grown talent—a scarce resource—within the community. Fourth, it encourages economic diversification and technological innovations by creating a climate that rewards productivity and innovation.

Communities must operate in a hypercompetitive environment. Appendix 3B, "Hypercompetition: America's 50 High-Tech Highways," provides a telling perspective on the intense competition for economic development and technological diversification. There may be as many as twenty thousand cities, states, and countries competing for less than one thousand relocations of high-tech firms. Consequently, cities and regions are focusing on building indigenous companies. They are trying to create a "Golden Triangle," "Satellite Alley," "Electronics Belt," "Robot Alley," "Tech Island," and "Silicon Bayou," all of which are attempting to link universities, government entities, and private corporations in new approaches to economic development.

To compete in this kind of environment, communities must stress factors that enhance quality *for* life. *For* implies a more proactive approach to insuring the quality of an economic region. It conveys a recognition of the economic importance of qualitative factors. Some of these are:

Quality of schools

Quality of parks and playgrounds

Outdoor recreational opportunities

Variety of entertaining activities

Cultural events

Relaxing ambience of community

Community safety

Community cleanliness

Ease of transportation within the city

Accessibility of airport

Housing costs

Availability of jobs for spouses

As a place to raise children

As a place to live

Climate

Air quality

By stressing these factors, communities can develop a linkage among key institutions to build a viable public–private infrastructure, a strong financial environment, a vibrant entrepreneurial spirit, and a commitment and dedication to risk taking.

Entrepreneurship Stimulants

A variety of social and economic factors are stimulating entrepreneurial activity and thus generating more robust economic development. These factors include an increasing focus on capital formation, changing institutional relationships, supportive government programs, a reassessment of intellectual property, and new approaches to innovations.

A growing pool of capital dedicated to the entrepreneurial process is being created in the United States today. Much of the attention concerning this pool has been focused on venture capital—a dynamic and creative process by which capital investments in midgrowth enterprises are made, managed, and developed. Venture capital is generally available only to firms with a proven track record. Venture capitalists rarely provide seed capital—that is, capital used to prove a concept, to build a prototype, or to permit an entrepreneur to start a new firm. Consequently, mechanisms are needed for entrepreneurs to reach a point where they may be in a position to tap the resources of the venture capital industry.

A second stimulator concerns the commercialization of technology through new institutional developments. The ability to transform scientific and technical developments into profitable business opportunities is at the heart of the commercialization process. There are institutions that directly perform research and development activities—government laboratories, industry, universities and colleges, and other nonprofit institutions. These institutions are looking for innovative ways to collaborate, to promote entrepreneurial activity, and to diffuse technology while they reap the rewards of their intellectual property assets. Each of these institutions holds potential entrepreneurs who are considering ways to commercialize their ideas.

A third stimulant to the entrepreneurial process is the proactive role of federal, state, and local governments. The federal government is actively seeking to fund and support technological efforts that have the potential for commercialization.

Fourth, universities, federal laboratories, industry, and research consortia are undertaking a major reassessment of policies and approaches to intellectual property due to hypercompetition. This is particularly important to many emerging high-technology companies. Since entrepreneurs are springing from each of these institutions to take their ideas and innovations to the marketplace, it is becoming more important to reassess questions concerning patents, licenses, royalties, and general ownership of scientific and technological developments. Given the growing collaborative relationships that are developing between business, government, and academia and given their more direct attempts to transfer technology to the marketplace, there is likely to be increasing numbers of entrepreneurs seeking the opportunity to commercialize their ideas and innovations.

A fifth stimulant to new business development is the removal of barriers to innovation through the establishing of an environment favorable to entrepreneurial activity. The removal of barriers has been accomplished on a variety of levels, including the federal, state, and local governments and by industry. On the national level, the federal government has encouraged the transfer of technology from federal laboratories and has encouraged research consortia formation by modifying antitrust laws. Many state governments have repealed tax laws considered disadvantageous to technology-oriented firms, have enacted special education laws to help keep and attract highly qualified personnel to local employment, and have endeavored generally to create an environment conducive to entrepreneurship. Many corporations, recognizing that entrepreneurship increases productivity, have established flexible corporate cultures to accommodate *intra*preneurial activity. Some have even established venture capital pools and incubator units to invest in entrepreneurially oriented employees.

New Business Incubator

Successful entrepreneurship takes a wide variety of talents. However, it is rare to find a potential entrepreneur who combines the technical expertise necessary for successful product commercialization. One concept developed since 1980 to facilitate the development of entrepreneurial creativity and education is the incubator unit.

Incubator units are designed to assist entrepreneurs in developing their business skills in an environment that simultaneously stimulates creativity. Although incubators vary in scope of assistance provided, there are some generic components to the incubator concept. An incubator provides low cost office and/or laboratory space, administrative services, access to library and computer facilities, skilled consultants, an inexpensive work force in the form of graduate and undergraduate students, and special contacts with bankers, venture capitalists, technologists, and government officials. In this environment, an aspiring entrepreneur is free to be technologically creative since his energies can be devoted to product development and not to the rigors of obtaining financing or managing an organization. During this time, the entrepreneur associates with other entrepreneurs facing similar difficulties, providing an association that should, it is hoped, stimulate the entrepreneur's drive for success and help solve problems. (See figure 3–1).

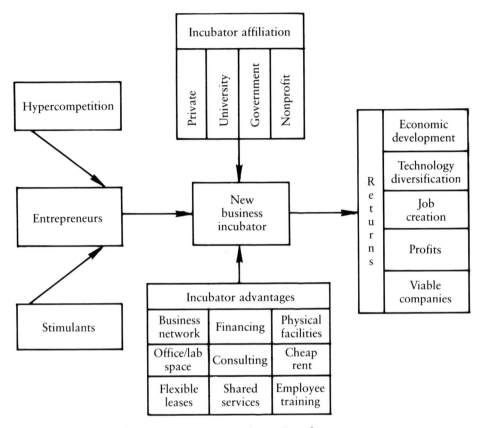

Figure 3–1. New Business Incubator

An incubator is not only an organization, but also a physical unit. Incubators start as a single building or group of buildings where the participating entrepreneurs can be housed and where, due to physical proximity, they will spontaneously interact. In the building, there may be space for a number of different entrepreneurs. The institution sponsoring the incubator will provide secretarial support, duplicating services, accounting services, technical editing help, computer equipment, conference space, health and other benefit packages, and access to university facilities and expertise for a nominal fee.

The advantages of being on or near a university campus are numerous: library facilities, exposure to state-of-the-art technical thinking and equipment, undergraduates that form a pool of cheap and technically skilled labor, a creative environment, and potential employment as a lecturer. Companies within the incubator profit from the technical resources of the university in a variety of ways, such as the best available talent when they need it without having to carry that high-priced talent on their payroll. These companies also receive the stimulus and catalytic effect associated with working alongside outstanding professionals from outside their organization.

Organizationally, incubators differ from one another due to their varying priorities, which are different because of the funding that supports the incubator unit. Funding sources include federal, state, and local governments, communities, universities, private individuals and foundations, and corporations. Incubators may be associated with any of these funding sources to varying degrees and, therefore, have similar goals but different priorities. The general goals of incubators are to develop firms, often technically based, and stimulate entrepreneurship. Incubators may seek to develop jobs, create investment opportunities for college endowments, expand a tax base for local government, enhance the image of college technical programs, speed transfer of technological innovation from the academic and research worlds to industry, fill a perceived gap in venture capital financing by improving the quality of locally based entrepreneurial talent, and build a core of indigenous companies.

The Entrepreneurial Network

Entrepreneurship is a dynamic process. As such it necessarily requires links to relationships not only among and between individuals but also among and between a variety of institutions. The stronger, more complex and more diverse the web of relationships, the more the entrepreneur is likely to have access to opportunities, the greater his chance of solving problems expeditiously, and ultimately the greater the chance of success for a new venture.

The entrepreneurial network, as depicted in figure 3–2, illustrates some of the potential links and relationships that can promote and sustain new ventures in an economic area. A university provides business and research centers, continuing business education (especially in management and marketing skills), and potentially a base for research and development, which also helps develop entrepreneurs. Major

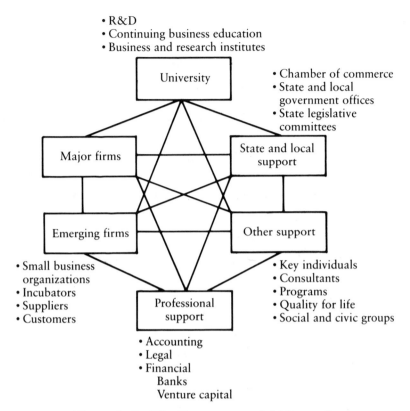

• R&D
• Continuing business education
• Business and research institutes

• Chamber of commerce
• State and local
  government offices
• State legislative
  committees

• Small business
  organizations
• Incubators
• Suppliers
• Customers

• Key individuals
• Consultants
• Programs
• Quality for life
• Social and civic groups

• Accounting
• Legal
• Financial
    Banks
    Venture capital

Figure 3–2. The Entrepreneurial Network

firms provide key credibility to emerging companies as customers and are sources of spin-off opportunities. Emerging firms provide a tier of peer support, find critical help in incubators, and establish important links with and through suppliers and customers. Professional support comes through networks to accountants, lawyers, and financiers. State and local governments provide incentives, direct aid, and access to contracts while responding to the creative pressures of emerging business interest groups. Other support networks take a variety of forms: key individuals, consultants, workshops and business education programs, social and civic groups, and collective efforts to improve quality for life factors.

Through networking, communities can advance economic development and technological diversification by providing a broader and richer range of opportunities to entrepreneurs.

Trends in Economic Development

There are seven major trends affecting the direction of economic development:[6]

1. Technology as a resource
2. Hypercompetition in domestic and international markets
3. The role of invention
4. Government as stimulator
5. Entrepreneurial and Intrapreneurial development
6. Innovative capital formation
7. Collaborative relationships

Technology is more than a thing, a gadget, or even a process. It is a self-generating resource that is not consumed in the process of use. Consequently, it is an important form of economic wealth.

Hypercompetition is forcing a reassessment of our individual and collective responses to the marketplace. Fierce domestic and international competition for scientific, technological, and economic preeminence is forcing communities and regions to leverage all their resources—human, technological and financial—to compete effectively for vibrant and diversified economies.

The United States is experiencing an unprecedented burst of invention. Myriad technological advances are occurring with incredible speed and frequency. The ability to commercialize these inventions will have direct and immediate economic consequences.

Federal, state, and local governments are trying to find positive noninterventionist approaches to encouraging entrepreneurship and technological diversification. They seek to create jobs, provide benefits to the small business sector, and push technology. The creation of an environment that promotes entrepreneurial activity has become a more important focal point in government policy development.

People with raw energy and a proclivity for risk taking built the

United States. They are continuing to build it today—in new ways, with new approaches. These entre- and intrapreneurs are breaking tradition and providing a dynamic source of creative and innovative enterprises.

Innovative capital formation is providing the catalyst for the entrepreneurial process. Mechanisms for providing seed capital as well as an expanding venture capital industry are helping to build new ventures. If the entrepreneurial process is to succeed, it is essential to continue to support and expand the formation of capital and its innovative utilization in new business development.

Finally, creative collaborative relationships are being formed between business, government, and academia. These ties are forging new opportunities for commercialization and are accelerating the technology transfer process.

Conclusion

Progress in economic development and technological diversification does not happen accidentally or haphazardly. In a hypercompetitive environment, the economic renaissance of an area depends on a city's or region's ability to address critical needs. To sustain the momentum of positive economic growth, communities must establish programs for investment in a viable public–private infrastructure. This includes not only meeting requirements for infrastructure needs such as roads, water, and utilities and services but also providing for educational needs and diversified cultural amenities.

A vibrant financial environment is essential to continued economic development. This includes a sophisticated banking community that understands the unique problems and needs of emerging companies, especially technologically based companies, and an expanding venture capital industry that can address the requirements of high-risk ventures. Only in this way can an area insure diversified opportunities for entrepreneurs.

A pool of capable people keeps economic development on track. A community, therefore, has to find ways to insure a locally trained workforce with a minimum reliance on imported services. As needs are supplied locally, there are more opportunities for entrepreneurs, including opportunities for minorities. A workforce with the know-how appropriate to community needs is essential for economic renaissance.

Technology venturing provides strategic direction for the economic renaissance of an area. It requires new relationships between business, government, and academia. It creates new institutional links. By responding to a rapidly changing environment, it engenders a dynamic entrepreneurial spirit.

Notes

1. George Kozmetsky, "Technology Venturing: The New American Response to the Changing Environment," in *Technology Venturing*, ed. Eugene B. Konecci and Robert L. Kuhn (New York: Praeger Publishers, 1985), pp. 3–13.

2. For further information on venture capital see George Kozmetsky, Michael D. Gill, Jr., and Raymond W. Smilor, *Financing and Managing Fast-Growth Companies: The Venture Capital Process* (Lexington, Mass.: Lexington Books, 1985).

3. *Target '90* (San Antonio, Tex.: Office of the Mayor, 1984).

4. *Technology and Growth: State Initiatives in Technological Innovation*, Final Report of the Task Force on Technological Innovation, Committee on Transportation, Commerce and Technology, the National Governor's Association, July 1983.

5. The presentation on entrepreneurial process, hypercompetition, entrepreneurship stimulants, and trends in economic development are extracted from Raymond W. Smilor and Michael D. Gill, Jr., *The New-Business Incubator: Linking Talent, Technology, Capital, and Know-How* (Lexington, Mass.: Lexington Books, forthcoming).

6. These trends have emerged from the research program and conference activities of the IC^2 Institute, University of Texas at Austin.

Appendix 3A
Selected University–Corporation Programs

Business Firm	Activity	Funding	Academic Institution
Monsanto Company	Biomedical proteins and peptides to regulate cellular functions—30 percent basic, 70 percent applied to human diseases	$23.5 million; 5-year renewable	Washington University St. Louis, Missouri
Monsanto Company	Will sponsor basic research in plant molecular biology structure and regulation of plant genes	$4 million; 5-year	Rockefeller University
IBM	Develop manufacturing engineering courses. 1981 IBM grants totaled $17 million.	$50 million; $10 million cash, $40 million equipment	Five universities share $10 million cash (to be announced). Twenty universities to receive the equipment. Includes University of Texas at Austin.
Green Cross Corporation (OSAKA)	Mass-producing monoclonal antibodies by all fusion techniques to combat cancer	$ unknown, 2-year contract signed	University of California
American Cyanamide–Lederle Labs	Pathway to generate chemical mediators causing allergic reactions to develop drugs to block released mediators	$2.5 million; 5-year grant	The Johns Hopkins School of Medicine

Appendix 3A *continued*

Business Firm	Activity	Funding	Academic Institution
W. R. Grace Company	Research in microbiology	$6–8 million; 5-year grant	MIT
Apple Computer to Xerox (26 companies)	Microelectronic innovations; 31 high-tech research projects	$2.2 million in cash and equipment	University of California, Microelectronic Innovations and Computer Research Opportunities Program. 6 U.C. campuses.
IBM	Robotics and use of computers and assembly lines	$1 million grant	University of Pennsylvania School of Engineering and Applied Science
NSF and coalition of some 30 industrial companies	Establish the University/Industry Cooperative Center for Robotics	$ unknown	Site: University of Rhode Island
Celanese Corporation	Specific basic bio-technology research	$1.1 million; 3-year term	Yale University
Bristol-Meyers Company	Developing anticancer drugs; company option to license cancer chemotherapy drugs discovered by participating Yale faculty	$3 million; 5-year cooperation agreement	Yale University
Gould Inc.	Gould Lab computer service facility	$500,000 over next 5 years	Brown University
IBM	NYU Robotics Center, math, geometric molding and software	Major contribution from IBM and equipment value unknown	New York University

NSF grant plus Carolina Power and Lights, Digital Equipment, Exxon, General Telephone & Electronic, IBM, ITT, Western Union, and Western Electric	North Carolina State's University/Industry Cooperative Research Center for Communications and Signal Processing. Basic and applied research.	NSF: $650,000; 5-year grant Industrial sponsors: $50,000 each for first 5 years	North Carolina University
Hoechst	Biotechnology research	$70 million over 10 years	Massachusetts General Hospital and Harvard University
Dupont	Genetic engineering	$6 million over 5 years	Harvard Medical School
Monsanto	Tumor angiogenesis factor	$23 million over 12 years	Harvard University
Engenics (consists of Bendix, General Foods, Koppers, Mean, MacLaren, and Elf Technologies)	Industrial microbiology	$1 million; 4 years	University of California at Berkeley and Stanford
Syntex and Hewlett-Packard	Biotechnology	$600,000 per year for 3 years	Stanford University
Exxon	Combustion research	$7–8 million; 10 years	MIT
Westinghouse	Robotics	$1.2 million per year	Carnegie-Mellon
Industry participants	Industry scientists work for a year at CalTech and get view of ongoing research and share expertise with faculty and staff	$100,000 each	CalTech
IBM, General Electric, and Norton	Research funds and equipment for a Center for Integrated Structures	So far: $1.25 million from GE for 3 years; Norton Co. donated building; and IBM provided a $2.75 million electron beam lithograph system	Rensselaer Polytechnic

Appendix 3A *continued*

Business Firm	Activity	Funding	Academic Institution
Consortium Caterpillar Tractor Company Cummins Engine Company John Deere Company United Technologies Research Center	Engine research includes diesel engines and fuel	$ unknown	MIT–Sloan Automotive Labs
MCC–Microelectronics and Computer Technology Corporation	MCC in Austin–Programs Long Range 1 cost-effective interconnection of computers using VLSI chips + $1 million + circuit elements 2 8–10 year advanced computer architecture study 3 breakthroughs in CAD/CAM systems 4 quantum improvement in procedures and tools centered on expert and knowledge-based system	MCC budget after startup $50 to $100 million per year	University of Texas at Austin and Texas A&M University

Source: Reprinted with permission from Eugene B. Konecci and Robert L. Kuhn, eds., *Technology Venturing* (New York: © Praeger Publishers, 1985), Appendix D, 224–226.

Appendix 3B
Hypercompetition: America's 50 High-Tech Highways

State	Area	Participants: Universities, Government Entities, Base Companies	Government Agency	Mature High-Tech Centers	Developing High-Tech Centers	Emerging High-Tech Centers
California	Santa Clara County, "Silicon Valley"	Stanford, Fairchild Camera & Instrument, Hewlett-Packard, Apple Computer, Intel, National Semiconductor	California Department of Economics and Business Development (Sacramento)	X		
	Orange County	University of California–Irvine, California State–Fullerton, Long Beach State University, North American Aviation, Ford Aeroneutronics, Baker International, Xerox, Cannon	Economic Development Corporation of Orange County (Irvine)		X	
	Sacramento	University of California–Davis, California State University at Davis, Hewlett-Packard, Signetics, Intel, Teledyne, Shugart	Sacramento Commerce and Trade Organization (Sacramento)		X	
	San Diego, "Golden Triangle"	University of California–San Diego, San Diego State University, Scripps Institute of Oceanography, General Dynamics, Rohr Industries	San Diego Economic Development Corporation (San Diego)		X	

Appendix 3B *continued*

State	Area	Participants: Universities, Government Entities, Base Companies	Government Agency	Mature High-Tech Centers	Developing High-Tech Centers	Emerging High-Tech Centers
Maryland	Montgomery County, "Satellite Alley"	COMSAT, Fairchild, Litton, IBM, NASA, NSA, National Institute of Health	Maryland Industrial Development Board (Annapolis)		X	
	Prince George County	University of Maryland–College Park, Litton, NASA, OAO, Martin Marietta	Prince George Economic Development Corporation (Landover)		X	
Massachusetts	Route 128–Boston	MIT, Harvard, Boston University, Tufts, Northeastern, DEC, Wang, Honeywell, GE, GTE, RCA, Raytheon	Massachusetts Department of Commerce and Development (Boston)	X		
Florida	Orlando area–"Electronics Belt"	Pratt & Whitney, GE, IBM, Westinghouse, Harris Corporation, Martin Marietta, Western Electric	Florida Division of Economic Development, Florida Department of Commerce (Tallahassee)		X	
	Dade, Broward, Palm Beach Counties, "Silicon Beach"	University of Miami	Florida Division of Economic Development, Florida Department of Commerce (Tallahassee)		X	
	Gainsville to Orlando– "Robot Alley"	University of Florida–Gainsville, IBM, GE, Westinghouse	Florida Division of Economic Development, Florida Department of Commerce (Tallahassee)			X

Building Indigenous Companies • 63

State	Region	Institutions/Companies	State Agency		
New York	Long Island–"Tech Island"	SUNY–Stonybrook, Polytechnic Institute of New York, Grumman Aerospace, Brookhaven National Labs, Cold Springs Harbor Labs, Harris Corporation	New York State Science & Technology Foundation (Albany)	X	
	Syracuse	Syracuse University, Carrier, GE, Research Corporation of Syracuse, Niagra Scientific	New York State Science & Technology Foundation (Albany)		X
Texas	Austin, San Antonio	University of Texas–Austin, University of Texas–San Antonio, Motorola, Lockheed, Tandem	Texas Industrial Commission (Austin)	X	
	Dallas–Ft. Worth–I-20	University of Texas–Dallas, University of Dallas, Texas Instruments, E-Systems, Sunrise Systems, Nuclear Medicine Labs	Texas Industrial Commission (Austin)	X	
	Houston–I-610 and I-45 to Woodlands	Texas A&M, Rice, University of Houston, Texas Medical Center, Litton, Shamrock, Visidyne, Switch Data, NASA, oil companies	Texas Industrial Commission (Austin)	X	
New Mexico	Rio Grande Research Corridor	New Mexico Tech, University of New Mexico, New Mexico State University, Intel, Motorola, Signetics, GTE, GE, Western Electric, Kirkland AFB, Los Alamos Labs, Sandia Labs, Sperry Rand	New Mexico Economic Development Division (Sante Fe)		X

Appendix 3B *continued*

State	Area	Participants: Universities, Government Entities, Base Companies	Government Agency	Mature High-Tech Centers	Developing High-Tech Centers	Emerging High-Tech Centers
Virginia	Fairfax County—I-95 and Washington	George Mason University, ATT Long Lines, GTE, McDonnell Douglas, Westinghouse	Fairfax County Economic Development Authority (Vienna)		X	
Ohio	Cleveland	Lewis Research Center (NASA), Defense Contract Administration, Case Western Reserve University, Picker International, Johnson & Johnson, TRW, Bendix	Department of Economic Development (Cleveland)		X	
	Columbus	The Ohio State University, Western Electric, Bell Labs, Rockwell International, Battelle Memorial Research Institute	State Department of Development (Columbus)		X	
	Cincinnati	University of Cincinnati, GE, Cincinnati Milicron, Structural Dynamic Research Corporation	Cincinnati Chamber of Commerce			X
	Dayton	University of Dayton, Wright State University, NCR, Mead, Wright-Patterson AFB, Air Force Institute of Technology, Monsanto Research, Bendix, Grumman	Dayton Development Council			X

State	Area	Companies/Institutions	Organization		
Pennsylvania	Philadelphia Route 202	University of Pennsylvania (Wharton), Drexel University, University City Science Center, IBM, Commodore	Technology Council, Chamber of Commerce (Philadelphia)	X	
	Pittsburgh	Alcoa, Pittsburgh Plate Glass, US Steel, Westinghouse, Gulf, University of Pittsburgh, Carnegie-Mellon	Commonwealth of Pennsylvania, Department of Commerce (Harrisburg)	X	
Washington	Seattle-Bellevue, I-5 corridor	University of Washington, Boeing, Eldec Corporation, John Fluke Company, Squibb, Weyerhauser	Department of Commerce and Economic Development (Olympia)	X	
Tennessee	Knoxville-Oak Ridge	University of Tennessee, Oak Ridge National Laboratories, Boeing, Goodyear Aerospace, Westinghouse, Magnavox	Tennessee Technical Foundation (Knoxville)		X
New Jersey	Princeton	Princeton University, RCA, Grumman Aerospace, American Cyanamid, Exxon, Mobile	New Jersey Department of Commerce and Economic Development (Trenton)	X	
Colorado	Colorado Springs	University of Colorado–Colorado Springs, Rolm, TRW, Ford Aerospace, Honeywell	Division of Commercial Development, State of Colorado (Denver)	X	
	Denver-Boulder	University of Colorado–Boulder, Colorado State University, DEC, NCR, Hewlett-Packard	Division of Commercial Development, State of Colorado (Denver)	X	

Appendix 3B *continued*

State	Area	Participants: Universities, Government Entities, Base Companies	Government Agency	Mature High-Tech Centers	Developing High-Tech Centers	Emerging High-Tech Centers
Illinois	Chicago	Northwestern University, University of Illinois, Illinois Institute of Technology, University of Chicago, Bell Labs, Western Electric, Amoco, Abbott Labs, Searle, Gould, Northrup, Fermi Labs, Argonne National Labs	Illinois Department of Commerce (Chicago)		X	
Alabama	Huntsville	University of Alabama–Huntsville, Redstone Arsenal, Intergraph Inc., Army Corps of Engineers, Army Missile Command, Lockheed, Rockwell, Boeing	Development Division of Chamber of Commerce (Huntsville)		X	
Arizona	Phoenix-Tempe	Arizona State University, Motorola, Sperry Rand, ITT, Intel, Goodyear, Honeywell, IBM	Arizona Office of Economic Planning and Development		X	
	Tucson	IBM, Hughes Aircraft, Anaconda Copper, National Semiconductor, University of Arizona–Tucson	Tucson Economic Development Corporation (Tucson)		X	

State	Location	Universities and companies	Development office			
Michigan	Ann Arbor	University of Michigan, Ford, GM, Chrysler, Bendix	Office of Economic Development, Department of Commerce (Lansing)			X
Louisiana	Lafayette, "Silicon Bayou"	University of Southwest Louisiana, Regional Vocational Technical School, Celeron, Shell, Texaco, NASA, Exxon	Lafayette Harbor Terminal and Industrial Development District (Lafayette)		X	
Minnesota	Minneapolis-St. Paul	University of Minnesota, 3M, Control Data, Honeywell, Cray Research	Minnesota High Tech Council (Minneapolis)		X	
Utah	Salt Lake City	University of Utah, Eaton, UNIVAC Aerospace, U.S. Steel, Kennecott Copper	Utah Economic Development Division (Salt Lake City)		X	
North Carolina	Raleigh-Durham-Chapel Hill, "Research Triangle"	North Carolina State University, University of North Carolina, Duke, IBM, Environmental Protection Agency, Becton, Dickenson, GE Semiconductor, Burroughs, Data General, Northern Telecom	North Carolina Department of Commerce, Industrial Development Division (Raleigh)	X		
Georgia	Atlanta	Georgia Tech, Rockwell, Scientific Atlanta	Office of the Governor (Atlanta)		X	
Rhode Island	Newport, Portsmouth, Middletown–Aquidneck Island	Naval War College, Brown University, University of Rhode Island, Raytheon Submarine Division, U.S. Navy Underwater Systems Center, Gould, Goodyear	Rhode Island Department of Economic Development (Providence)			X

Appendix 3B *continued*

State	Area	Participants: Universities, Government Entities, Base Companies	Government Agency	Mature High-Tech Centers	Developing High-Tech Centers	Emerging High-Tech Centers
Indiana	Indianapolis	Purdue, Indiana University, GM, Eli Lilly, Renault, International Harvester, Naval Avionics Center	Office of the Mayor (Indianapolis)		X	
Wisconsin	Madison	University of Wisconsin–Madison, University of Madison Hospital, GE Medical Systems, Ohio Medical Labs, Nicolet Instruments, Cray Research	Wisconsin Department of Development (Madison)			X
Oregon	Tualatin Valley—"Sunset Corridor," west of Portland	Tektronix, Intel	Oregon Business and Community Development Department (Salem)		X	
	Wilmette Valley–I-5 Portland to Eugene	Oregon State University, Hewlett-Packard, Spectra Physics	Oregon Business and Community Development Department (Salem)		X	
	Bend-Richmond	Bend Research	Economic Development Department (Salem)			X
South Carolina	Columbia	Monsanto, GE, Sony, United Technologies, NCR, DEC	State Development Board of South Carolina (Columbia)			X

State	Area	Companies/Institutions	Agency		
Oklahoma	entire state	Western Electric, GM, oil companies, University of Oklahoma, Norman, Oklahoma State University, Tinker AFB	State Department of Economic Development (Oklahoma City)		X
New Hampshire	Salem-Manchester-Nashua–"Golden Triangle"	University of New Hampshire, Lowell University, DEC, Bedford Computer, Sanders Associates, Kollsman Instruments, Computer Vision, Data General	New Hampshire Office of Industrial Development (Concord)	X	
Arkansas	Little Rock to Pine Bluff–Technology Corridor	University of Arkansas–Pine Bluff and Little Rock, Little Rock Medical Center, BEI Electronics, Pine Bluff Arsenal, National Center for Toxicological Research	Arkansas Industrial Development Commission (Little Rock)		X
Maine	Portland	University of Southern Maine, Data General, DEC, Fairchild Semiconductor, Sprague Electric	Maine State Development Office (Augusta)		X
Vermont	Burlington	University of Vermont, GE, IBM, DEC, McDonnell Douglas, Bendix	Vermont Economic Development Department (Montpelier)		X

Source: Reprinted with permission from Eugene B. Konecci and Robert L. Kuhn, eds., *Technology Venturing*, (New York: © Praeger Publishers, 1985), Appendix C, 215–223.

4

Entrepreneurship and Intrapreneurship: Methods for Creating New Companies That Have an Impact on the Economic Renaissance of an Area

Robert D. Hisrich

Economic development involves more than just increasing per capita output and income. It also involves initiating and constituting change in the structure of business and society. This change is accompanied by growth and increased output, which allows more to be divided by the various claimants. What in an area facilitates the needed change and development? One theory of economic growth depicts innovation as the key not only in evolving the new products (or services) for the market but stimulating investment in the new ventures created, thereby expanding productive capacity. This new investment works on both the demand and supply sides of the growth equation: the new capital created expands the capacity for growth (supply side) and the new spending created utilizes the new capacity and output (demand side).

Yet despite the importance of investment and innovation in the economic development of an area, there is still lacking an adequate understanding of the product evolution process, the process by which innovation develops and commercializes, and how the results of entrepreneurial activity stimulate economic growth.

The product evolution process is indicated in figure 4–1 as a cornucopia, the traditional symbol of abundance. It begins with knowledge in science, thermodynamics, fluid mechanics, electronics, and technology and ends with products or services available for purchase in the marketplace.[1] The critical point in this process is the intersection of knowledge and a recognized social need, the beginning of the product development phase. This point, labeled *iterative synthesis*, often fails to evolve a marketable innovation.

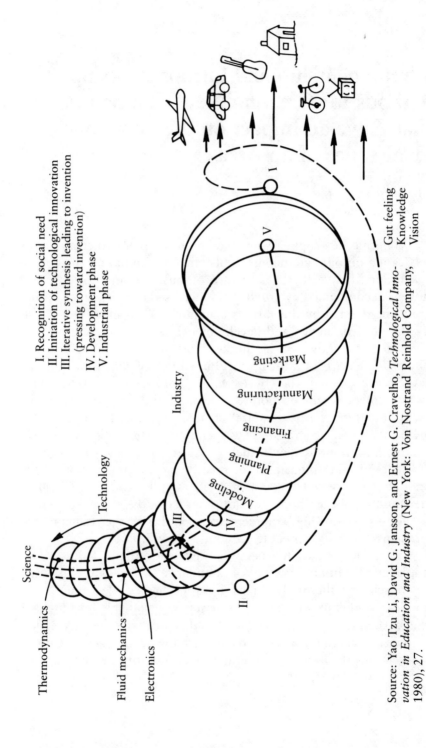

I. Recognition of social need
II. Initiation of technological innovation
III. Iterative synthesis leading to invention
   (pressing toward invention)
IV. Development phase
V. Industrial phase

Gut feeling
Knowledge
Vision

Figure 4–1. Product Evolution

Source: Yao Tzu Li, David G. Jansson, and Ernest G. Cravelho, *Technological Innovation in Education and Industry* (New York: Von Nostrand Reinhold Company, 1980), 27.

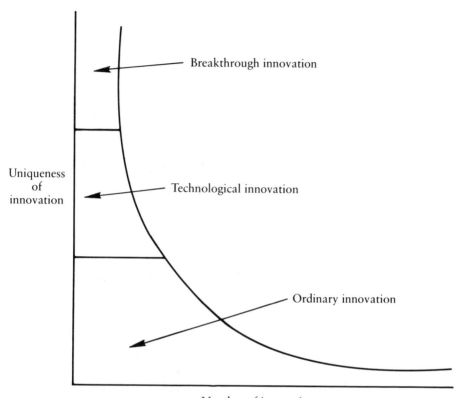

Figure 4–2. **Types of Innovations**

The innovation at this juncture can of course be of varying degrees of difference. As is indicated in figure 4–2, the largest number of innovations introduced on the market are ordinary innovations—ones having little difference or technology. These are followed in terms of decreasing number and increasing technology by technological innovations and breakthrough innovations. Each of these innovations (particularly the latter two types) often evolves and develops to commercialization through a product planning and development process.

Although the product planning and development process varies from industry to industry, as well as from firm to firm within a given industry, its activities generally follow the pattern indicated in figure 4–3. The process is divided into five major stages: idea stage, concept

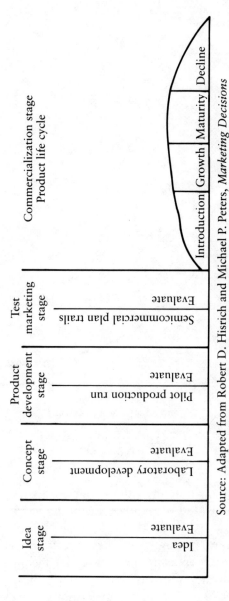

Source: Adapted from Robert D. Hisrich and Michael P. Peters, *Marketing Decisions for New and Mature Products* (Columbus, Ohio: Charles E. Merrill Publishing Co., 1984).

Figure 4–3. Product-Planning and Development Process

stage, product development stage, test marketing stage, and commercialization.[2]

In the idea stage, suggestions for new products are obtained from all possible sources: customers, competition, R&D, distribution, and company employees. Frequently, one of the creative problem-solving techniques discussed below are used to develop marketable ideas. The suggested ideas need to be carefully screened to determine which are good enough to qualify for a more detailed investigation. Established objectives and defined growth areas provide a basis for developing these screening criteria.

Ideas passing the initial screening enter the concept stage, where they are developed into more elaborate product concepts. In evaluating the product concept, the company's strengths and weaknesses and the needs of potential buyers must be taken into consideration. A business plan indicating the product features and a marketing program should be developed and a sample of potential buyers should be asked to evaluate the concept.

Once the new product concept has been approved, it is further developed and refined into a prototype and tested. This is the product development stage, where the technical and economic aspects of the potential new product are assessed by assigning specifications for the development process to members of research and development. Unless excessive capital expenditures make it impossible, laboratory-tested products should be created and produced on a pilot run basis, allowing for production control and product testing. The potential products can then be evaluated by in-use consumer testing to determine whether they have features superior to products currently available.

Although the results of the product development stage can form the basis of the final marketing plan for the new product, a market test can be undertaken to increase the certainty of successful commercialization. This last step in the evaluation process—the test marketing stage—provides actual sales results indicating the acceptance level by consumers. Of course, positive results cannot guarantee success, however, they do indicate the degree of probability of a successful launch.

The extent of the evaluation in each stage of the product planning and development process depends to a great extent on the product, market, and competitive situation as well as the costs involved in the time elapsing between idea generation and commercialization. The long time period in the product planning and development process must be carefully weighed against the costs associated in the evaluation process and the costs of commercialization. Even though 90 percent of available ideas are eliminated, the idea and concept stages still take very little time and money—only about 10 percent of the total time and expenditures involved in the entire product planning and development process. The product development stage requires about 30 percent of the total expenditures and 40 percent of the total time. On the other hand, the test marketing stage takes 12 percent of the total money and 20 percent of the time. In the commercialization stage, about 50 percent of the total expenditures occur in only 23 percent of the total time.[3] Regardless of the time and cost tradeoffs it makes, a company still has to actively develop sources for new product ideas so that the product planning and development process can continually lead to commercialization.

How can the product planning and development process more effectively lead to commercialization and the gap between science and the marketplace be bridged? By three mechanisms: government, existing businesses, or formation of new businesses.

Government

The government is one source for commercializing the results of the interaction between a social need and technology. This is called technology transfer and has been the focus of a significant amount of effort and research. Despite all the effort and findings, to date few inventions resulting from scientific research though technologically sound have reached the commercial market. Most of these by-products have little application to any social need, and the few that do require significant modification to have market appeal. Though the government has the financial resources to successfully transfer any technology to the marketplace, it lacks the necessary business skills, particularly marketing and distribution, to successfully commercialize. In addition, government bureaucracy and red tape often prohibit the necessary strategic business from being formed in a timely manner.

Intrapreneurship

The second mechanism—existing businesses—can also bridge the gap between science and the marketplace. These companies have the ex-

Table 4–1
Characteristics of an Intrapreneurial Environment

Organization operates on frontiers of technology

New ideas encouraged

Trial and error encouraged

Failures allowed

No opportunity parameters

Resources available and accessible

Multidiscipline teamwork approach

Long time horizon

Volunteer program

Appropriate reward system

Sponsors and champions available

Support of top management

---

isting financial resources, business skills, and usually the marketing and distribution system to successfully commercialize a new invention. Yet, too frequently the bureaucratic structure, the emphasis on short-term profits, and a highly structured organization inhibit creativity and new products being developed. Corporations recognizing these inhibiting factors and the need for creativity and inventions have attempted to establish an intrapreneurial spirit in their organizations. What is this intrapreneurial spirit and intrapreneurship? It is entrepreneurship within an existing business structure.

In establishing a successful intrapreneurial environment, certain factors and leadership characteristics must be operant in the firm.[4] The overall characteristics of a good intrapreneurial environment are summarized in table 4–1. The first is that the organization operates on the frontiers of technology with new ideas being encouraged. Since R&D is a key source for successful new product ideas, this area must operate on the cutting edge of the technology of the industry. New ideas must be encouraged and supported not discouraged as frequently occurs in firms where rapid return on investment and high sales volume requirements exist.

Second, experimentation—trial and error—must be encouraged. New products or services do not instantaneously appear. It took time and some product failures before the first marketable computer appeared. A company wanting to establish an intrapreneurial spirit has to establish an environment that allows and even encourages mistakes and failures. Although this is in direct opposition to the established corporate career and promotion system, without the opportunity to fail few if any corporate intrapreneurial ventures will succeed. Almost every entrepreneur has experienced at least one failure before establishing a successful venture.

Third, an organization should make sure there are no initial opportunity parameters inhibiting free creative problem solving. Frequently, various turfs are protected, frustrating attempts by potential intrapreneurs to establish new ventures. In one Fortune 500 company the attempt at establishing an intrapreneurial environment ran into problems and eventually failed when the potential intrapreneurs were informed that a proposed product was not possible because it was in the domain of another division.

Fourth, the resources of the firm must be available and easily accessible. As one intrapreneur stated: "if my company really wants me to take the time, effort, and career risks to establish a new venture then it needs to put money and people resources on the line." Insufficient funds often are allocated to the task of creating something new, with resources instead being committed to solving problems that have immediate impact on the bottom line. Even when funds are available, all too often the reporting requirements make it so difficult to obtain these resources that frustration and dissatisfaction result.

Fifth, a multidiscipline, teamwork approach needs to be encouraged. This open approach with participation by needed individuals regardless of area is the antithesis of corporate organizational structure and theory. Yet, in evaluating successful cases of intrapreneurship, one key to the success was the "skunkworks," or business transactions involving key people occurring outside the corporate structure. Perhaps some companies can facilitate internal venturing by merely legitimizing and formalizing the "skunkworks" already occurring. Developing the needed teamwork approach is further complicated by the fact that a team member's promotion and overall career within the corporation is related to performance in his current position, not his contribution to the new venture being created.

In addition to encouraging teamwork to start the venture, the corporate environment must establish a long time horizon for evaluating the success of the overall program and the success of each individual venture. If a company is unwilling to invest money with no expectation of return for five to ten years, then it should not attempt to create an intrapreneurial environment. This patient money in the corporate setting is no different from the investment–return time horizon used by venture capitalists and others in the risk capital market when investing in an entrepreneurial effort.

Sixth, the spirit of intrapreneurship cannot be forced on individuals; it must be on a volunteer basis. There is a difference between corporate thinking and intrapreneurial thinking, with individuals being much better on one side of the continuum. The majority of managers in a corporation are not capable of being intrapreneurs. This self-selection of participants must be coupled with the latitude for each participant to carry a project started through to completion. This is not in line with most corporate procedures for new product introduction where different departments and individuals are involved in each stage of the development process. An individual willing to spend the excess hours and effort to create a new venture, must have the opportunity to carry the project to completion. An intrapreneur falls in love with the venture and will do almost anything to ensure that success results.

Seventh, the intrapreneur needs to be appropriately rewarded for all the energy and effort expended in the creation of the new venture. Broad performance goals should be established with the intrapreneur receiving rewards based on meeting these goals. An equity position in the new venture is the best reward for motivating the amount of activity and devotion needed for success.

Eighth, a corporate environment favorable for intrapreneurship has sponsors and champions throughout, who not only support the creative activity and any failures but who have the planning flexibility to establish new objectives and directions. As one intrapreneur stated: "For a new business venture to succeed the intrapreneur needs to be able to alter plans at will and not be concerned about how close they are to achieving the previously stated objectives." Corporate structures frequently measure managers on their ability to come in close to plan, regardless of the quality of performance reflected in this accomplishment.

Finally, and perhaps most importantly the intrapreneurial activity must be wholeheartedly supported and embraced by top management. Top management must have a long time horizon and support the effort

Table 4–2
Intrapreneurship Leadership Characteristics

Understands the environment
Visionary and flexible
Creates management options
Encourages teamwork
Encourages open discussion
Builds a coalition of supporters
Persists

by physical presence as well as making sure the personnel and financial resources are available. Without top management supporting the effort, a successful intrapreneurial environment cannot be created.

Within this overall corporate environment, there are certain leadership characteristics needed. As summarized in table 4–2, these include: understanding the environment, being visionary and flexible, creating management options, encouraging teamwork while employing a multidisciplined approach, encouraging open discussion, building a coalition of supporters, and persisting.

In order to understand the environment, an intrapreneur needs to be creative. Creativity, perhaps at its lowest level in large corporations, tends, in general, to decrease with age and education. In order to successfully establish a new business venture, creativity and broad understanding of the internal and external environment must be present.

The person who is going to establish a successful new business venture must also be a visionary leader—a person who dreams great dreams. Although there are many definitions of leadership, the one that best describes the needed intrapreneurial leadership is: A leader is like a gardener. When you want a tomato, you take a seed, put it in fertile soil, and carefully water under tender care. You don't manufacture tomatoes, you grow them. Martin Luther King said, "I have a dream," and thousands followed in spite of overwhelming obstacles. In order to establish a successful new business venture the intrapreneurial leader must have a dream and work against all obstacles to achieve it.

The third characteristic is that the leader must be flexible and create management options. An intrapreneur does not mind the store but is playful and irreverent. By challenging the beliefs and assumptions of the corporation an intrapreneur has the opportunity of creating something new.

The intrapreneur must encourage teamwork and use a multidisciplined approach. This violates the organizational practices taught in most business schools and end up being incorporated in the established corporate structure. In every new company formation a broad range of business skills are needed: engineering, production, marketing, and finance. Using these skills in forming a new business venture usually requires crossing the established departmental structure and reporting systems. To minimize any disruption caused, the intrapreneur must be a good diplomat.

In developing a good team for creating something new, open discussion must always be encouraged. Many corporate managers have forgotten the frank, open discussions and disagreements that were a part of their educational process and spend time building protective barriers in their corporate empires. A successful new business venture can only be formed when the team involved feels the freedom to disagree and break down an idea until the best solution is reached. The degree of openness obtained depends on the degree of openness of the intrapreneur.

Openness is one factor leading to the establishment of a strong coalition of supporters and encouragers. The intrapreneur must encourage and affirm each team member particularly during the problem times. This encouragement is very important as the usual motivators of career paths and job security are not operational. A good intrapreneur makes everyone a hero.

Finally, but not least important, is persistence. Several times throughout the establishment of the new business venture frustration and obstacles will abound. Only by persistence on the part of the intrapreneur will successful commercialization result.

Underlying the environmental and leadership characteristics necessary for increasing intrapreneurship in a corporation is to develop creativity and generate new ideas. This can in part be facilitated through the use of creative problem-solving techniques.

Creative Problem-solving Techniques

Creativity is an important attribute of every intrapreneur. Unfortunately, creativity declines with age and lack of use. Creativity declines

Table 4–3
Creativity and Problem-solving Techniques

Brainstorming
Reverse brainstorming
Synectics
Gordon method
Check list method
Free association
Forced relationships
Collective notebook method
Heuristics
Scientific method
Kepner-Tregoe method
Value analysis
Attribute listing
Morphological analysis
Matrix charting
Sequence-attribute modification matrix
Inspired (big dream) approach
Parameter analysis

when a person starts to attend school, becomes a teen, becomes thirty, and becomes fifty. In addition, the latent creative potential of an individual can be stifled by perceptual, cultural, emotional, and organizational factors. One method for unlocking creativity and generating creative ideas and innovation is to employ one or more of the creative problem-solving techniques indicated in table 4–3.[5]

Brainstorming

Brainstorming is probably the most well known and widely used of the creativity and problem-solving techniques. It is an unstructured process for generating—through spontaneous contributions of participants—all possible ideas about a problem within a limited time frame. Although the technique can be used by individuals, it is primarily an organized group process. A good brainstorming session starts with a carefully prepared problem statement that is neither too broad (which would diversify ideas too greatly so that nothing specific would emerge) nor too narrow (which would tend to confine responses).[6]

Once the problem statement is prepared, group members are chosen with the ideal group size being six to twelve people. It is important that the group comprise a wide range of knowledge and that no supervisor–subordinate relationships are involved. When group members are experts in the field dealing with an extremely familiar issue, the resulting range of new ideas is usually severely restricted.

After careful planning, the brainstorming session consists of the following six stages:

1. State the problem and discuss it for familiarity and background.
2. Restate the problem.
3. Write down the restatement responses for all to see.
4. Start a warm-up session to get participants freewheeling, laughing, and generally in the mood for brainstorming.
5. Conduct the actual brainstorming session.
6. Come up with the wildest idea.

Participants must never criticize or evaluate during the brainstorming session. All ideas, no matter how illogical, must be recorded.

After the close of the session each participant must receive a complete list of the generated ideas as soon as possible. The list is organized into related areas to facilitate suggestions for implementation from the group members.

Reverse Brainstorming

Reverse brainstorming is similar to brainstorming, except that criticism is allowed. In fact, the technique deliberately tries to find fault by asking the question, "In how many ways can this idea fail?" Because participants are critical of each other's suggestions, the leader must be careful to maintain the group's morale. Reverse brainstorming often is used prior to brainstorming or other creative techniques to initiate innovative thinking.[7] The process most often involves the identification of everything wrong with the issue at hand followed by a discussion of ways to overcome these.

Synectics

Synectics is a creative process that forces participants to consciously apply, through analogy, preconscious mechanisms to solve problems. In this method a group works through two steps. The first step is to make the strange familiar. This involves basic analysis that enables the group, through the use of generalizations or models, to put the problem into a readily acceptable or familiar perspective, thereby eliminating the strangeness.

Once the strangeness is eliminated, participants engage in the second step, a reversal of the first, making the familiar strange in order to seek novel solutions. Each one of four mechanisms of analogy (personal, direct, symbolic, and fantasy) is used to discuss the success of the proposed solution.[8]

Gordon Method

The fourth method—the Gordon method—unlike many other creative problem-solving techniques, begins with group members not knowing the exact nature of the problem, ensuring that the solution is not clouded by preconceived ideas and thought patterns.[9] The Gordon method relies heavily on a group leader, who is the only one in the usual three-hour session aware of the actual problem. A session begins with the leader mentioning an associated concept that is general in nature. The group begins by conceiving and expressing a number of ideas. Then a concept is developed, followed by related concepts, with guidance by the group leader. The actual problem is then revealed, enabling the group to make suggestions for implementation or refinement of the final idea.

Check List Method

In the check list method, a list, composed of related issues or suggestions, is prepared and a problem is analyzed. Participants use the list of questions or statements to guide the direction or the ideas. The check list aids participants in concentrating on specific areas and may be specialized or generalized and of any length as indicated in the example below:[10]

Put to Other Uses? New ways to use as is? Other uses if modified?

Adapt? What else is like this? What other ideas does this suggest? Does past offer parallel? What could I copy? Whom could I emulate?

Modify? New twist? Change meaning, color, motion, odor, form, shape? Other changes?

Magnify? What to add? More time? Greater frequency? Stronger? Larger? Thicker? Extra value? Plus ingredient? Duplicate? Multiply? Exaggerate?

Minify? What to substitute? Smaller? Condensed? Miniature? Lower? Shorter? Lighter? Omit? Streamline? Split up? Understated?

Substitute? Who else instead? What else instead? Other ingredient? Other material? Other process? Other power? Other place? Other approach? Other tone of voice?

Rearrange? Interchange components? Other pattern? Other layout? Other sequence? Transpose cause and effect? Change pace? Change schedule?

Reverse? Transpose positive and negative? How about opposites? Turn it backward? Turn it upside down? Reverse roles? Change shoes? Turn tables? Turn other cheek?

Combine? How about a blend, an alloy, an assortment, an ensemble? Combine units? Combine purposes? Combine appeals? Combine ideas?

The questions help clarify the problem and usually work best when the problem is familiar.

Free Association

One of the simplest techniques in creative problem solving, which can be used in groups or by individuals, is free association. This technique is used to stimulate the thinking process to elicit an entirely new slant to a problem. To begin the process, a word or phrase related to the problem is written down, then another, and another. Each new word adds something fresh to the ongoing thought processes, thereby creating a chain of ideas. Free association is best used in instances where no structure is required and no specific output desired.

Forced Relationships

Forced relationships is a creative problem-solving technique that asks questions about objects or ideas in an effort to determine what new object or idea would result from a new combination being made. The new concept is developed through a five-step process:[11]

1. Isolate the elements of the problem.
2. Find the relationships among these elements.
3. Record the relationships in an organized fashion.
4. Analyze the record of relationships to find ideas or patterns.
5. Develop new ideas from these patterns.

Collective Notebook Method

In the collective notebook method of creative problem solving, a notebook is prepared that includes a statement of the problem, blank pages, and any pertinent background data.

Each participant receives an identical copy of the prepared notebook and agrees to review the problem, think about its solution, and record ideas several times a day, for at least one month. At the end of the month each individual prepares a list of the best ideas, suggestions for future thoughts and research, and other new ideas unrelated to the original problem.[12]

Notebooks are then given to a central coordinator who synthesizes the data and summarizes all the material. The summary becomes the topic of a final creative discussion by the group.

This method lends itself to groups of varying sizes—including very large ones—and to problems with wide scopes. It is heavily dependent, however, on the synthesizing ability of the coordinator, who brings the multiple suggestions into focus for final discussion.

Heuristics

Heuristics is a method of independent problem solving that relies solely on the individual's propensity to indulge in the art of discovery through progression of thoughts, insights, and learning. Heuristics is probably used more in business applications than one might imagine simply because business managers most often settle for a plausible estimate of the outcome of a decision rather than on any assured certainty.

Although heuristics has many specific applications in creative problem solving, one approach is called the heuristic ideation technique (HIT).[13] The process involves locating all relevant concepts that could be associated with a given product area and generating a set of all possible combinations of ideas.

Scientific Method

The scientific method, widely used in various fields of inquiry, consists of principles and processes required in any investigation. These include steps for developing rules for concept formation, followed by conducting observations and experiments, and finally validating the hypothesis. The approach involves (1) defining the problem; (2) analyzing the problem; (3) gathering and analyzing data; (4) developing and testing potential solutions; and (5) choosing the best solution.

Kepner–Tregoe Method

The Kepner–Tregoe method is a creative problem-solving technique for analyzing problems in a group setting.[14] Since the method isolates or finds a problem and then decides what should be done about it, the final decision is made after several iterations. The method lends itself very well to made-to-order situations, with each member of the group receiving an assignment.

Value Analysis

Another creative problem-solving technique—value analysis—develops methods for doing something that will maximize its value to the firm.[15] This method uses a question such as "Can this part be of lesser quality, since it isn't a critical area for problems?" To implement a value analysis procedure, regularly scheduled meetings must be established to develop, evaluate, and refine ideas.

Attribute Listing

Attribute listing is an idea-finding technique that requires individuals to list the attributes of an item or problem and then look at each from a variety of viewpoints. Modification occurs in this process as each attribute suggests possible new uses to participants.[16] In this way, the method brings originally unrelated objects together to form a new combination that better satisfies a need.

Morphological Analysis

Morphological analysis attempts to look at all possible combinations of variables in solving a problem. First the problem is stated and broadly defined; then all the conceivable solutions are listed in a model. Finally the suggested solutions are evaluated through the aid of a model.[17]

Matrix Charting

Matrix charting is a systematic method for searching for new opportunities by listing elements along both axes of a chart and then asking basic questions regarding these elements. The answers are then recorded in the relevant boxes of the matrix. The basic questions used to elicit creative responses are: what can it be used for? Where can it be used? Who can use it? When can it be used? How can it be used?[18] The matrix includes as many boxes as the ideas or elements present.

Sequence-Attribute Modification Matrix (SAMM)

The sequence-attribute modifications matrix (SAMM), which is more effective in group settings, identifies areas of evaluation but does not provide actual solutions. This approach centers around developing a matrix that indicates on the left-hand side a sequence of activities and on the right-hand side possible modifications to the process. Each activity is evaluated and necessary modifications determined.

Big-Dream Approach

The big-dream approach requires the individual to dream great dreams about a problem; that is, to think big. Then every possible subject related to the big-dream idea is investigated. Once this step is completed, a second big-dream idea is similarly researched and so on until the dream is molded into a workable form.[19]

Parameter Analysis

A final method, which is useful in creative problem solving and developing new ideas, is a parameter analysis.[20] Parameter analysis is a matching process involving two aspects—parameter identification and creative synthesis. In step one (parameter identification), variables in the situation are analyzed to determine which are most important to the problem's solution. These variables become the focus of the investigation with the other variables being set aside. After the primary issues have been identified, the relationships between parameters that most effectively describe the underlying issues are examined.

Following an evaluation of the parameters and relationships, the development of the solution(s) occurs. This step (creative synthesis) involves a total understanding of the problem so that a unique product can be developed.

Entrepreneurship

The final method for bridging the gap between science and the marketplace—entrepreneurship—is the process of creating something different with value by devoting the necessary time and effort, assuming the accompanying financial, psychological, and social risks, and receiving the resulting rewards of monetary and personal satisfaction.[21]

Many entrepreneurs have difficulty bringing their innovations to the market due to lack of managerial skills, lack of finances, need to modify the unmarketable innovation, lack of knowledge of the product planning and development process, and lack of marketing skills, particularly in the area of distribution.

Entrepreneurship and the accompanying entrepreneurial process resulted in several million new businesses being formed throughout the world even in controlled economies such as China, Hungary, and Poland. Although the exact number is unknown, estimates indicate that in the United States (which leads the world in company formation) from nine hundred thousand to 1.85 million new companies were formed in 1984.

Indeed, millions of company formations occur despite recession, inflation, high interest rates, lack of infrastructure, economic uncertainty, and the fear of failure. Each of these company formations is a very personal human process that, although unique, has some com-

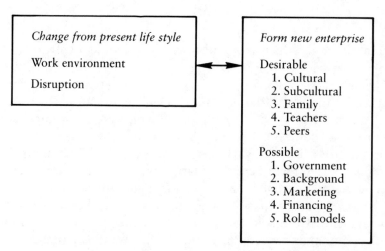

Figure 4–4. Decisions for a Potential Entrepreneur

mon characteristics. Like all processes it entails movement from something to something—movement from a present life style to forming a new enterprise, as indicated in figure 4–4.

The decision to leave a present career and life style is indeed not an easy one. It takes a great deal of energy to change and create something new. Individuals tend to start businesses in familiar areas. Two work environments tend to be particularly good in spawning new enterprises: R&D and marketing. Working in technology (R&D), individuals develop new product ideas or processes and often leave to form new companies when their new ideas are not accepted by present employers. Similarly, individuals in marketing become familiar with the market and customer's unfilled wants and needs and frequently start new enterprises to fill these needs.

Perhaps even more stimulation to leave a present life style and overcome the inertia by creating something new comes from a negative force—disruption. A significant number of company formations occur among people who have retired, whose spouse has moved, or who have been fired. There is probably no greater force than personal dislocation to galvanize one into action. A study in one major city in the United States indicated that the number of new business listings in the Yellow Pages increased by 12 percent during a layoff period. Another cause of disruption and resulting company formation is the completion of an educational degree. For example, a student who does not receive a promotion upon completing an M.B.A. degree may decide to start a new company.

What causes this change due to the work environment or disruption to result in a new company being formed instead of something else? The decision to start a new company occurs when an individual perceives that it is both desirable and possible.

The perception that starting a new company is desirable results from an individual's culture, subculture, teachers, family, and peers. A culture that values an individual who successfully creates a new business will spawn more company formations than one that does not. For example, the United States places a high value on being your own boss, individual opportunity, being a success, and making money—all aspects of entrepreneurship. Therefore, it is not surprising to find a high rate of company formation in the United States. On the other hand, in other countries successfully establishing a new business and making money is not as highly valued and failure is a disgrace. If a person in these countries succeeds some would remark, "It must be something crooked," or, if a new enterprise fails, the remark would be, "Thanks be to God that nothing worse happened—it was expected." It is easy to understand why fewer companies are spawned in this type of culture.

However, even an entire culture is not totally for or against entrepreneurship. Many different subcultures that shape value systems are operant within a cultural framework. There are pockets of entrepreneurial subcultures in the United States, such as Route 128, Silicon Valley, Dallas–Ft. Worth–Austin, the North Carolina Triangle, and Tulsa. These subcultures support and even promote entrepreneurship—forming a new company—as one of the best occupations. It is not surprising that more students, faculty, and individuals actively think about and plan to form new enterprises in these supportive environments.

There are of course variations within these cultures caused by family differences. Studies of companies in a variety of industries throughout the United States and the world indicate that the founders of companies who have fathers and/or mothers who were independent businesspersons is between 50 percent and 72 percent. The independence that results from being company owners, professionals, artists, or farmers permeates the entire family, giving encouragement and value to company formation activity.

This individual, a product of his or her culture, subculture, and family, is further influenced by teachers, peers, and other respected individuals. Teachers can significantly influence individuals regarding not only business careers in general but company formation as one possibility. Schools with exciting courses in entrepreneurship and innovation tend to spawn entrepreneurs and can actually drive the entrepreneurial environment in an economic area. A look at Route 128 and MIT; Silicon Valley and Stanford; North Carolina Triangle and the University of North Carolina; and Dallas–Ft. Worth–Austin and the University of Texas proves this point. Strong educational undergirding is a prerequisite for entrepreneurial activity and company formation in an area. Peers are also important. An area with an entrepreneurial pool and meeting place where entrepreneurs and potential entrepreneurs meet and discuss ideas, problems, and solutions spawn more new companies.

Their desire to form a company that is generated from the culture, subculture, family, teachers, and peers of course needs to be present before action is taken that results in a company being formed. What makes it possible to form a new company? Several factors—government, background, marketing, role models, and finances—contribute to the possibility of creating a new venture (see table 4–1). The government contributes to the possibility by providing the infrastructure needed to support a new venture. It is not surprising that more companies are formed in the United States given the roads, utilities, economic stability, and transportation available versus that available in other countries. Even the tax rate for companies and individuals in the United States is better than in countries such as Ireland, Italy, or England. Countries that have a repressive tax rate, particularly for individuals, can suppress company formation since the monetary gain cannot be achieved even though the social, psychological, and financial risks are present.

The entrepreneur then must have the background needed to make the company formation possible. Knowledge from formal education and previous business experience makes a potential entrepreneur feel capable of forming and managing a new enterprise. Individuals tend to start businesses in fields in which they have worked. In many cases, the idea for a new company occurs while the individual is still working in his or her present position. Educational systems also are important in providing the needed knowledge of business and engineering. Indeed, entrepreneurs are not born they are developed.

Marketing also plays a critical role in the possibility of forming a new company. Not only must a market of sufficient size be available for the new idea but the marketing know-how of putting together the best total package of product, price, distribution, and promotion is needed for successful product launching. A company is more easily formed in an area where there is market demand not technology push.

Perhaps one of the most powerful influences making company formation seem possible are role models. To see someone else do something and succeed makes it easier to picture yourself doing a similar activity, of course better. A frequent comment of entrepreneurs regarding their motivations for starting their new venture is: "If that person who is so stupid can do it, so can *I*."

Finally, financial resources are needed to form a new company. Companies are formed when financial resources are readily available. Although the majority of the start-up money for any new company comes from personal savings, credit, friends, and relatives, there is a need for seed capital (capital up to $100,000) to help spawn new companies. Each venture has a common trait—the need for risk capital. Risk capital investors play an essential role in the development and growth of entrepreneurial activity. When seed capital is readily available more new companies form.

What are the types of start-ups formed from this entrepreneurial decision process? Although there are many classification systems, one that is most useful for economic development purposes divides start-ups into three categories: life-style firms, foundation companies, and high-potential ventures. A life-style firm is privately held and usually achieves only modest growth due to the nature of the business, the objectives of the entrepreneur, and the limited (if any) money devoted to research and development. This type of firm may grow after several years to thirty–forty employees with annual revenues of about $2 million. A life-style firm primarily exists to support the owners and has little opportunity for significant growth and expansion.

The second type of start-up—the foundation company—is created from R&D and lays the foundation for a new industry. Such a firm can grow in five to ten years to forty to four hundred employees and $10 million to $30 million in yearly revenues. Since this type of start-up rarely goes public it draws the interest of private investors but not the venture capital community.

The final type of start-up—the high-potential venture—is the one that receives the greatest investment interest and publicity. The company may start out like a foundation company, but its growth is far more rapid. After five to ten years, the company could have around five hundred employees with $20–$30 million in revenue. With such growth and revenues, the high-potential start-up venture frequently will go public or be purchased by a larger company.

Given that the decision-making process needs to appear desirable and possible in order for an individual to change from a present life style to a new one, it is not surprising that the 163,051 new business formations in the first quarter of 1985 varied throughout the United States. As indicated in figure 4–5, seven of the nine census regions had increases in new incorporations; the record total (163,051) was up 1 percent from a previous high of 161,389 in the same three months of 1984. New England had the largest increase (4.6 percent) followed by East North Central (up 4.3 percent), South Atlantic (up 3.8 percent), West South Central (up 3.5 percent), and East South Central (up 3.1 percent). The two regions having decreases in incorporations were the Pacific states declining 9 percent and the farm-belt states (West North Central region) declining 8.9 percent.

The Entrepreneur

Who is this entrepreneur who is behind this overall record of new business formations? The concept of entrepreneurship is an evolving one with the term *entrepreneur* stemming from a French word meaning "between-taker" or "go between." From early references in the Middle Ages and eighteenth century economists such as Richard Cantillon, the entrepreneur and entrepreneurship process have been investigated from various vantage points: economic, sociological, cultural, and managerial. The highlights in the development of this understanding are listed in table 4–4. As indicated in the table, the idea that the entrepreneur is different from the person supplying capital emerged, followed by the notions of risk taking, creating, and innovating, until the overall concept evolved that was discussed in the previous section.

Throughout this development of theory, a profile of the male and female entrepreneur has emerged, which is indicated in tables 4–5 and 4–6. The male entrepreneur tends to have independently employed parents, and to be the first-born child in the family, college educated, married, self-confident, and desirous of independence. He has a high

Slight increase in incorporations

Seven of the nation's nine Census Bureau regions reported small increases in new business incorporations, according to a Dun & Bradstreet study comparing the first quarter 1984 & 1985.

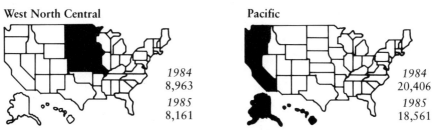

South Atlantic–E

1984
40,242

1985
41,754

New England

1984
7,918

1985
8,285

East South Central

1984
6,301

1985
6,496

Middle Atlantic

1984
28,909

1985
29,442

West South Central–E

1984
15,440

1985
15,978

East North Central

1984
21,181

1985
22,097

Mountain

1984
12,029

1985
12,277

West North Central

1984
8,963

1985
8,161

Pacific

1984
20,406

1985
18,561

Source: The Associated Press, *Tulsa World*, 31 August, 1985, 19.
Note: E = estimated.

Figure 4–5. Incorporations in Geographic Areas in the United States

Table 4–4
Development of Entrepreneurship Theory and Term *Entrepreneur*

Stems from French; means *between-taker* or *go-between.*

Middle Ages: actor (warlike action) and person in charge of large-scale production projects.

17th century: person bearing risks of profit (loss) in a fixed price contract with government.

1725: Richard Cantillon—person bearing risks is different from one supplying capital.

1797: Beaudeau—person bearing risks, planning, supervising, organizing, and owning.

1803: Jean Baptiste Say—separated profits of entrepreneur from profits of capital.

1876: Francis Walker—distinguished between those who supplied funds and received interest and those who received profit from managerial capabilities.

1934: Joseph Schumpeter—entrepreneur is an innovator and develops untried technology.

1961: David McClelland—entrepreneur is an energetic moderate risk taker.

1964: Peter Drucker—entrepreneur maximizes opportunities.

1975: Albert Shapero—entrepreneur takes initiative, organizes some social–economic mechanisms, and accepts risk of failure.

1980: Karl Vesper—entrepreneur seen differently by economists, psychologists, business persons, and politicians.

1983: Gifford Pinchot—intrapreneur is an entrepreneur within an already established organization.

1985: Robert Hisrich—entrepreneur is the process of creating something different with value by devoting the necessary time and effort, assuming the accompanying financial, psychological, and social risks and receiving the resulting rewards of monetary and personal satisfaction.

tolerance for ambiguity and a high energy level and, in his early 30s, starts his first significant venture in an area of previous experience.

The percentage of businesses started and operated by women is less than those started by men, however, the number is increasing at a rapid rate. For example, the number of female sole proprietorships was 3,104,029 or 22 percent of all sole proprietorships, according to the Internal Revenue Service, whereas the Bureau of Labor statistics indicates that between 1974 and 1984 the number of self-employed women grew 74 percent or six times faster than self-employed men.

Who is this female entrepreneur? She is the first-born child of

Table 4–5
Profile of a Male Entrepreneur and His Business

First-born child

Father and/or mother in independent business

College-educated

Married

Early 30's for first significant venture

Previous experience in new venture

Desires independence

Self-confident

Moderate risk taker

High tolerance for ambiguity

High energy level

Biggest problems in start-up:
  Obtaining seed capital
  Marketing

Biggest problems in current operations:
  Cash flow management
  Weak collateral position

Table 4–6
Profile of a Female Entrepreneur and Her Business

First-born child of middle-class parents

Liberal arts degree

Married

Middle 30's for first significant venture

Motivated by desire for independence and job satisfaction

Small and young business

Biggest problems in start-up:
  Lack of business training
  Obtaining credit

Biggest problems in current operations:
  Lack of experience in financial planning
  Weak collateral position

middle-class parents, at least one of whom is independently employed, she has a close relationship with her father and, after obtaining an undergraduate and frequently a graduate degree in some area of liberal arts, marries, has children and starts her first significant entrepreneurial venture in the service area in her late 30s or early 40s. Her biggest problems at start-up and later in the venture reflect a lack of business training and generally are in the financial area.

Enterprise Development Center

One method for facilitating the formation of new businesses and helping economic development of an area is the enterprise development center. The enterprise development center established at the University of Tulsa brings together federal, state, and city governments, engineering and business schools, businesses, venture capital firms, financial institutions, and potential inventors and entrepreneurs in developing and forming new companies. The center contains five major aspects: the intrapreneurship center, the venture capital exchange, the innovation center, the incubation center, and a workplace (see figure 4–6). The intrapreneurship center researches and helps established companies create the needed intrapreneurial spirit and environment discussed above in order to facilitate the formation of new companies within the parent company. Through this effort established businesses can have a positive impact on the economic growth of an area by creating new companies under the corporate umbrella. Given the assets of the established companies, this is one of the fastest methods for having a positive impact on the economy of an area.

The second aspect of the enterprise development center—the venture capital exchange—provides the needed seed capital for a new company. Since this is the focus of chapter 5 in this book, it is unnecessary to elaborate on this part of the center except to indicate that providing an information transfer mechanism between entrepreneurs and angels (seed capital investors) and matching mutual interests helps provide the needed finances that makes the company formation process possible.

The innovation center—the third aspect—provides assistance to entrepreneurs and potential entrepreneurs. This assistance includes technological evaluation, entrepreneurial assessment, commercial fea-

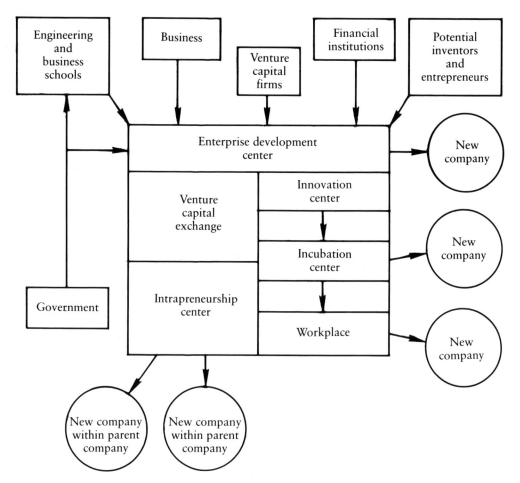

Figure 4–6. The Enterprise Development Center

sibility studies, and product development and modification, resulting in a license to another company, a new company in an incubation center or workplace, or a new company being formed in the actual business environment (see figure 4–7). The innovation center focuses on helping the entrepreneur create the needed business plan (see table 4–7).

The final two aspects of the enterprise development center—the incubation center and workplace—provide the needed protective environment for a start-up company to survive and grow. Probably the approach to economic development that is currently attracting the

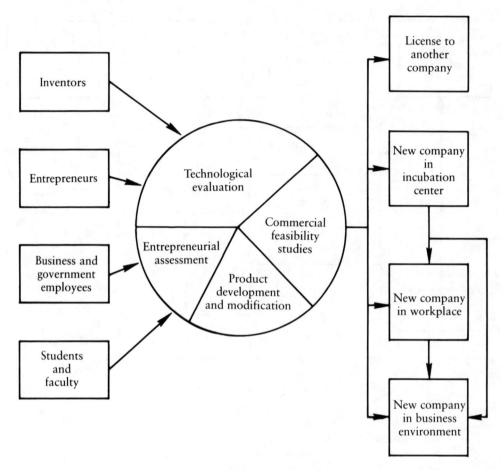

Figure 4–7. Innovation Center

most widespread attention is the new business incubator. The incubator is a significant link for the success of a new business because it provides the protective environment and support so needed, as is discussed in chapter 3 in this book. Although the 117 incubators throughout the United States vary in terms of their objectives and services provided, in general each incubator is designed to assist an entrepreneur in developing business skills and a company in a supportive environment. Most incubators provide some level of services and assistance. The services generally include low-cost office, laboratory, warehouse, and/or manufacturing space, secretarial services (word

Table 4–7
Business Plan Outline

Cover sheet
  Name of business
  Names of principals
  Address and telephone number of business

Statement of purpose (executive summary)
  Description of business—product or service
  Business structure
  Description of:
    Amount of money being requested
    How funds will be used
    How funds will be repaid

Marketing plan
  The industry
  The competition
  Market size and opportunity
  Market segments served
  Marketing mix
  Key factors to success in market

Financial plan
  Sources and applications of funds
  Capital equipment list
  Balance sheet
  Break-even analysis
  Income statements
  Pro-forma cash flow statements

Organizational plan
  Location of business
  Organizational structure
  Management
  Nonmanagement personnel

Summary
  Application and expected effect of loan on business

Supporting documents (as required)
  Personnel resumés
  Job descriptions
  Credit reports
  Letters of reference
  Copies of contracts
  Copies of leases
  Copies of letters of intent
  Legal documents
  Production requirements

Source: Reprinted by permission of the publisher, from Robert D. Hisrich and Candida G. Brush, *The Woman Entrepreneur: Starting, Financing, and Managing a Successful New Business* (Lexington, Mass.: Lexington Books, D.C. Heath and Company, Copyright 1986), 64.

processing, typing, photocopying, receptionist, clerical, and filing), administrative services (mailing, accounting, equipment rental, billing, and contract administration), access to library and computer facilities, inexpensive graduate and undergraduate student assistance, consulting services (general management, marketing, financial, loan packaging, accounting, and legal), and a network of bankers, venture capitalists, technologists, and government officials. In this supportive environment, the entrepreneur can grow and nurture the company, ultimately leaving the incubator for the workplace or the general business environment.

The workplace concept is more prevalent in the United Kingdom and Ireland and is similar to the shared-office concept that is operational in the United States. In one respect, the workplace is an incubator without all the services. The workplace provides low-cost space and a minimum of secretarial services such as typing, photocopying, and receptionist. As such, it bridges the gap for a company that does not require the full range of services found in the incubator but is not quite financially strong enough to survive in the general business environment.

An enterprise development center is just one alternative to having a positive impact on the economic development of an area. Of more importance is that the political leaders of the city, state, or region recognize that a viable and perhaps best method for economic development is internal. This recognition needs to be followed by tangible monetary display and support and pooling of the government, university, business, and foundation resources available in the area to help present companies to survive and grow and new companies to form. A spirit of entrepreneurship and intrapreneurship needs to be the driving force in the area.

Notes

1. The process is discussed in Yao Tzu Li, David G. Jansson, and Ernest G. Cravelho, *Technological Innovation in Education and Industry* (New York: Van Nostrand Reinhold, 1980), 27–30.

2. This process is described in detail in Robert D. Hisrich and Michael P. Peters, *Marketing Decisions for New and Mature Products* (Columbus, Ohio: Charles E. Merrill, 1985), 156–178.

3. These times and cost estimates are presented in *Management of New Products* (New York: Booz, Allen and Hamilton, 1968), 10.

4. For a thorough discussion of the factors important in intrapreneurship see Rosabeth Moss Kanter, *The Change Masters* (New York: Simon and Schuster, 1983), 127–306; and Gifford Pinchot III, *Intrapreneuring* (New York: Harper & Row, 1985), 195–312.

5. A discussion of each of these techniques can be found in Robert D. Hisrich and Michael P. Peters, *Marketing Decisions for New and Mature Products* (Columbus, Ohio: Charles E. Merrill, 1984), 131–146.

6. For a discussion of this aspect, see Charles H. Clark, *Idea Management: How to Motivate Creativity and Innovation* (New York: ANA Com, 1980), 47.

7. For a discussion of this technique, see J. Geoffrey Rawlinson, *Creative Thinking and Brainstorming* (New York: John Wiley & Sons, 1981), 124, 126; and W. E. Souder and R. W. Ziegler, "A Review of Creativity and Problem-Solving Techniques," *Research Management* 20 (July 1977): 35.

8. For a thorough discussion and application of this method, see W. J. Gordon, *Synetics: The Development of Creative Capacity* (New York: Harper & Row, 1961), 37–53.

9. This method is discussed in J. W. Haefele, *Creativity and Innovation* (New York: Van Nostrand Reinhold, 1962), 145–147; Sidney J. Parnes and Harold F. Harding, *A Source Book for Creative Thinking* (New York: Charles Scribner's Sons, 1962), 307–323; and Souder and Ziegler, "Review of Creativity and Problem-Solving Techniques," 34–42.

10. Alex F. Osborn, *Applied Imagination* (New York: Scribner Book Companies, 1957), 318.

11. Rawlinson, *Creative Thinking and Brainstorming,* 52–59.

12. For a thorough discussion of the collective notebook method, see Haefele, *Creativity and Innovation,* 152.

13. See Edward M. Tauber, "HIT: Heuristic Ideation Technique," *Journal of Marketing* 36 (January 1972): 58–70.

14. For a discussion of this method and its application to the business environment, see Charles Kepner and Benjamin Tregoe, *The Rational Manager* (New York: McGraw-Hill, 1965), 39–56; and Charles Kepner and Benjamin Tregoe, "Developing Decision Makers," *Harvard Business Review* 38 (September–October 1960): 115–124.

15. For a discussion of value analysis and its application at General Electric, see "A Study on Applied Value Analysis," *Purchasing* 56 (8 June 1959): 63–65; and "The 20 Keys to Value," *Purchasing* 46 (8 June 1959): 66–67.

16. Parnes and Harding, *Source Book for Creative Thinking,* 308.

17. The process involved in using morphological analysis can be found in C. S. Whiting, *Creative Thinking* (New York: Reinhold, 1958), 63; and

Souder and Ziegler, "Review of Creativity and Problem-Solving Techniques," 38.

18. Charles H. Clark, *Idea Management: How to Motivate Creativity and Innovation* (New York: AMACOM, 1980), 47.

19. For a discussion of this approach, see M. O. Edwards, "Solving Problems Creatively," *Journal of Systems Management* 17 (January–February 1966): 16–24.

20. The procedure for parameter analysis is thoroughly discussed in Li, Jansson, and Cravalho, *Technological Innovation in Education and Industry*, 26–49, 277–286.

21. For a discussion of this and other concepts of entrepreneurship, see Robert D. Hisrich and Candida G. Brush, *The Woman Entrepreneur: Starting, Financing, and Managing a Successful New Business* (Lexington, Mass.: Lexington Books, 1985), 1–18.

Part III
Role of Venture Capital
in Economic Development

5

Role of Venture Capital in the Economic Renaissance of an Area

Barry M. Davis

Venture Capital Industry in the United States

Venture capital can best be characterized as a long-term investment involving the creation of early-stage companies, the expansion and revitalization of existing businesses, and the financing of management buy-outs of existing divisions of major corporations or privately owned businesses. The venture capitalist participates through equity involvement in the portfolio company, the direct purchase of stock, or a number of different financing methods. In addition, the venture capitalist is actively involved in the monitoring of portfolio company progress by bringing experience in investment and financial planning skills to the table. The venture capital process is characterized by a balanced risk–reward analysis, intensive analysis and investigation, individual structuring and tailoring of each investment opportunity, and direct value-added assistance through substantial commitments of time and experience to the portfolio company.

The organized venture capital community has been evolving since the early 1960s. The venture capital industry is a broad-based and highly successful investment medium. Its financial return to investors has greatly exceeded those of stocks and bonds over the past decade. The industry today is comprised of three types of companies: (1) private venture capital firms, (2) small business investment companies (SBICs), and (3) subsidiaries of major corporations.

Private venture capital companies have become the dominant sources of classic venture capital activity. Most of these firms are private limited partnerships with two to four general partners and are funded by insurance companies, pension funds, bank trust departments, corporations, wealthy individuals, and foreign investors. There are approximately 150 private venture capital companies in the United States.

The second major type of venture capital companies are small business investment companies. SBICs were created as a result of the enactment of the Small Business Investment Company Act of 1958 with the explicit purpose of providing long-term equity capital and management assistance to small and medium size businesses. SBICs have been acknowledged as the pioneers of the venture capital industry and were a major factor contributing to building a formalized venture capital industry. There are 383 SBICs operating in the United States. A counterpart to SBICs are minority enterprises small business investment companies (MESBICs), which provide capital exclusively to minority businesses. There are 144 MESBICs in the United States.

The third type of venture capital company was formed as subsidiaries of major corporations. Approximately one hundred major financial institutions and corporations have formed venture capital subsidiaries, such as First Chicago Corporation, Citicorp, Allstate Insurance Company, Xerox, Exxon, and General Electric.

Total size of the venture capital industry pool has grown from $2.5 billion in 1977 to over $16 billion in 1984. A key factor affecting this dramatic growth was the capital gains tax reduction in 1978.

Although $16 billion is a record high for the industry, the venture capital industry is still small in comparison with other capital resources in the United States. Pension funds, which have been a leading supplier of capital to private venture capital firms, have contributed almost $2 billion to the venture capital development process, and this $2 billion represents only 0.2 percent of total pension fund assets.

Philosophy and Objectives of a Venture Capital Firm

To understand venture capital, one needs to understand the philosophy that drives the venture capital firm. The objective of a venture capital firm is to generate long-term capital appreciation through debt and equity investment in small and medium size businesses. Even though the venture capitalist assists in the creation of jobs and the economic development of businesses within a region, the important driving factor is the realization of substantial capital gains.

In most instances, venture capitalists do not seek control of a company. They make their decision on the people on the management team and the rationale of the business and then support that management team. While control is not essential in a given deal, the investment agreement does provide a mechanism for the venture capitalist to step in to protect his investment if the deal is in trouble.

While venture capitalists expect to be on the board of directors, they still expect the management team to direct the company. Venture capitalists support and supplement management with dollars, financial and planning skills, experience, and guidance.

Each investment by a venture capitalist in a portfolio company is a long-term association with that company. There must be a basic, inherent trust between the venture capitalist and the entrepreneur. They must rely on each other. There must be no surprises. The company and the venture capitalist must be able to share the good news and the bad news. It is incumbent on the venture capitalist to be able to handle the bad news as well as the good. The venture capitalist must help the company make decisions to grow and develop over the long term. This requires patience balanced with a drive for success.

The relationship chemistry between the venture capitalist and the entrepreneur is of paramount importance. The venture capitalist must be able to brainstorm ideas, problem solve, and lend a veteran shoulder. The venture capitalist must be available to the entrepreneur to discuss problems and strategic planning issues while being a source of comfort and advice.

The venture capitalist must develop the trust with the entrepreneur and give assurance that there will be no armchair decision making, no second guessing. The venture capitalist should not mandate, but should suggest. On the other hand, the entrepreneur should have an open mind, be open to suggestions, and evaluate suggestions presented. The final decision rests with the company.

It is imperative that the goals and objectives of management and the venture capital firm be similar. When these goals and objectives diverge, the "green eye" syndrome develops. The entrepreneur begins to question the venture capitalist and some jealousy develops. Simultaneously, the venture capitalist begins to question why he did the deal originally. The relationship slowly begins to deteriorate. Parallel goals and objectives and the ability to pull in the same direction results in a healthy entrepreneur–venture capital relationship.

Before a venture capitalist invests in a given business, substantial due diligence and research has been performed, resulting in an ultimate understanding of the business. Thereafter, the venture capitalist must do the necessary homework in order to provide input at the board of directors' meetings. In addition to understanding the drives and motivation of management, the venture capitalist must know the market, the industry, and the unique niche that the company is pursuing.

The venture capitalist expects individuals on the management team to have substantial commitment to the company. This commitment must be reflected in invested dollars so that staying power will occur even in tough times. Since a venture capitalist has no desire to take over a company, a substantial commitment by management is essential in this process.

There are three primary objectives in the venture capitalist's determination to make an investment:

1. The company must have strong management; people with solid experience, balanced life styles, and spousal support are backed. Venture capitalists want bright, capable people with scrambling abilities who can meet special challenges.

2. The individual investment opportunity must be unique with a differential advantage with respect to competition. The company must have a special niche. Uniqueness of opportunity may come from the product, service, or the talent of the management team.

3. The individual investment opportunity must have significant capital appreciation.

Confidentiality in every investment deal of a venture capitalist is essential. The management team must be able to speak with frankness and candor, having the confidence that the information is treated with absolute confidentiality.

Business plans also are essential in obtaining venture capital. A business plan is the starting point in screening deals. It must have a clear-cut mission with objectives clearly stated and must be accompanied by an in-depth industry and market analysis. The upside potential and the downside risk must be presented.

Various types of companies can utilize venture capital dollars: (1) established companies with proven track records having a need for growth or expansion dollars and often a need for supplemental financing to the bank; (2) turnaround companies with solid management, a bright future, and a total commitment to the company by the management team, the banks, and other company creditors; and (3) start-up situations that are mirror images of previous experiences. These start-ups represent the greatest challenge and risk and normally the greatest reward.

In addition, venture capital dollars are frequently used for management buy outs and acquisitions. The benefits of a buy out are many. The sellers of the company are able to get cash or deferred payment. The key management is able to participate in ownership with the identity of the organization being maintained in most cases. Venture capital dollars in buy outs enable a large company to sell a division and provide liquidity for estate planning for privately held firms.

After twenty years in the industry, I am firmly convinced that the management counseling and advice are as important as the money the venture capitalist provides. Running a business is a lonely job.

The venture capitalist can advise on additional financing and bank relationships, mergers and acquisitions, preparations of budgets and forecasts, and performance of financial analysis. In addition, the venture capitalist should assist in management evaluation, not only in the continuing analysis of personnel but also in the search, screening, and selection of future management team members. Also, assistance should be provided in the investment banking function in contacts with the investment community.

The funds are usually provided by the venture capitalist through a combination of long-term debt and equity capital. Various instruments such as convertible debentures, convertible preferred stocks, subordinated debentures with warrants, common stock, or a combination of these are used to meet a company's needs and to provide a measure of income. The amount of equity contributed by the entrepreneur is based on the maturity of the company, its general financial condition, cash flow analysis, the amount of capital required, and the risk–reward profile.

Role of Venture Capital and Value Added to Growth Companies

In a growth company, the role of a venture capitalist involves more than simply supplying capital to develop and market an idea. Analysis of the idea from both a business and technical perspective should be provided as well as help in validating the risk–reward considerations of the business plan. Assistance should be provided in locating and developing a highly qualified technical and managerial team, obtaining investment capital, and meeting short-term and long-term financing needs. The role, then, of the venture capitalist is to serve as a support mechanism for innovative entrepreneurs in growth companies. A measure of this support is the number of value-added services and benefits a venture capitalist brings to the emerging growth company.

First, venture capitalists analyze the management team of a growth company, looking for compatibility among the team members and the balance of their personalities and skills. The entrepreneur is assisted in developing the proper balance of people to insure the success of a company. Too few people may result in weakness and too many in disruption and having the wrong people in the jobs may produce conflicts.

As the company grows, the venture capitalist must continually assist in the determination and selection of key people. The evaluation of job skills and people skills is becoming an increasing necessity to facilitate the success of a growth business. This includes the evaluation of incentives and rewards for individual performance. Individual fulfillment and development is a high priority in a growth company.

Second, the venture capitalist must receive a constant updating of the strategic plan. The strategic plan must contain clear-cut mission and objectives, and appropriate job descriptions and tasks for each key member of the team. The company must always be conscious of the market, therefore, market research is becoming more essential for effectively understanding the market and competitive issues. Since the strategic plan is the road map to success, the venture capitalist must continually probe and ask questions and assist in measuring the performance of the strategic plan.

Third, venture capitalists must assist the growth company in expanding in an orderly manner. The management of a company must never "bet the flagship." Orderly, sequential growth over time is essential. A growth company must never step backward in its corporate development. Company growth and expansion must be highly focused on cash flow disciplines. Cash flow is the lifeblood of growth business. Presently there is a return to the fundamentals of business—cash flow management and not merely the perception of value.

Fourth, the venture capitalist must continually bring clinical objectivity and a detached point of view to the growth business. Since the management team is constantly enmeshed in the day-to-day operation of a business, the "forest for the trees" concept has caused many businesses to fail. This clinical objectivity will assist the company in its ability to anticipate changes in the business climate. The company must deal with reality and adjust its management style to its changing needs and those of the marketplace.

Finally, venture capitalists must bring the discipline of business values, ethics, and a code of conduct to the growth business. Business reputation and an honest and straightforward manner in dealing with its customers must be ever present in the minds of a company's management team.

The Venture Capital Process

The venture capital process has been identified as both an art and a science. The art comes from the intuition, the gut feel, the creative aspects of the venture capital process. The science is involved with the systematic approach, data gathering, assessment, analysis, and disciplined risk–reward assessment.

The venture capital process really starts with the investment philosophy of the venture capital firm. What is the number and portfolio mix of start-ups, expansion companies, and management buy out opportunities? It starts with the decisions on the types of industries and the geographic region desired. It involves the analysis of the strategic plan of the venture capitalist concerning the product and industry specializations. It is involved with the management analysis in the assessment of the product and the idea, which is carried forward into the due-diligence process involving the in-depth analysis of the people accompanying the idea, the product, and the industry. Finally, the financing required is analyzed.

The venture capital process can be broken down into four steps. The first step is preliminary screening. This begins with a check of the files to determine if the deal or similar deals have been previously evaluated. Is the proposal consistent with the investment philosophy, both on a long-term policy and short-term cash needs of the venture capital firm? Is there appropriate portfolio balance? What is the view of the economy in the particular industry? Does the venture capitalist have a specific knowledge of the project? Are the numbers in the ball park? Does it meet return on investment criteria? Is there an indication of mutual trust and integrity in the principals? Is there a clear-cut strategic plan and does that plan make sense? Does the management appear capable? Do we believe that a long-term relationship is possible?

The second step is an agreement on principle terms. It is essential to get a basic understanding of the principal terms at an early stage of the process before a major commitment of time is made in the due-diligence process.

Detailed review and due diligence is the third step. Precise information must be obtained on the history, the business plan, detailed resumes of the individuals, industry research, financial history, customers, upside potential, and downside risk. There must be a thorough evaluation of the markets, the industry, financial analysis, customers, and management checks.

The final step is approval. A comprehensive, internal investment memorandum is prepared. This document reviews the venture capitalist's findings as well as the investment terms and conditions that will lead to a final decision enclosing the transaction.

Venture Capital and Economic Revitalization

Many states such as Oklahoma are at major crossroads in their history in regard to their ability to mandate and control economic development and growth over the foreseeable future. Citizens of such states want their states to become growth-oriented and to continue in that tradition.

Economic revitalization is a topic of great concern. There are certain fundamentals that relate to the ability of a city and state to prosper into the 1990s. There appears to be an emerging consensus in the realization that both education and economic development issues must be priorities and that a consistent growth plan for the future must be developed.

Recruitment and retention are key issues. Recruitment must involve bringing in to a state outside industries and growth-oriented companies. Equally as important is the retention and support of existing industries and the creation and development of new and emerging growth companies. An environment of entrepreneurial creativity and activity must be created.

Entrepreneurial support is mandatory. A city must claim a new title—the entrepreneurial capital. A city should be a center for ideas in a business hub of activity. It must couple its quality of life and living conditions with an environment of support for emerging growth companies. New informal relationships between business and education should be formed. Educational facilities from primary through secondary to college should establish a mandate of excellence. New relationships between the private sector and the public sector should be fostered. A master plan must be agreed on and all entities must work toward its obtainment. Citizens must be fully informed on the key issues of education and training, research and scientific potential, the business image of the city and state, and the methods of financing and supporting growth companies.

The Business Plan

The business plan is the most critical starting point of any business. It allows the entrepreneur to organize plans for both the near term and the long term. It allows the business objectives in the mission to be clarified. A SWOT exercise that analyzes the strengths, weaknesses, opportunities, and threats of a given business plan is often performed by a venture capitalist. The business plan allows the entrepreneur to analyze particular capabilities and the market niche of the business and to define the growth strategy and potential, money required, and particular niche of his product or service.

An important element of the business plan is the Executive Summary, which summarizes the management, marketing, competition, product, market differentiation, financial upside potential, and downside risk. A business plan contains the following elements:

Discussion of the management team. This should contain the resumes, references, educational background, job descriptions, and descriptions of the skills and talents each one of the principals brings to the venture.

Detail of the product or service. This should be a discussion of the product or service, analysis of the customers, technical risks, the patent possibilities, and so forth.

Marketing and sales. Who is the competition? What are their strengths and weaknesses? What is the pricing theory and market philosophy? What is the size of the market? A description of the market should be included.

Financial information. This section should contain pro forma financial data, cash flow projections, balance sheets, and a capital expenditure plan. Assumptions supporting each forecast, the amount of money needed, and the use of the proceeds must be indicated.

Additional information. This includes risk assessments, product brochures, market research information, references, and any other relevant industry information.

Characteristics of an Entrepreneur

Before starting a business, an entrepreneur needs to understand his or her personal characteristics. Each should go through a substantial soul searching to be sure that he or she has the capabilities to deal with the pressure. A venture capitalist would rather have a first-rate individual and a second-rate idea. The entrepreneur must have the adequate commitment, motivation, and skills to start and build a business. Strengths and weaknesses should be assessed before starting a business. The entrepreneur must determine if the management team has the necessary complementary skills necessary to succeed. Some key characteristics of a successful entrepreneur are:

Motivator. An entrepreneur must build a team, keep it motivated, and provide an environment for individual growth and career development.

Self-confidence. Entrepreneurs must have belief in themselves and the ability to achieve their goals.

Long-term involvement. An entrepreneur must be committed to the project with a time horizon of five to seven years. No ninety-day wonders are allowed.

High energy level. Success of an entrepreneur demands the ability to work long hours for sustained periods of time.

Persistent problem solver. An entrepreneur must have an intense desire to complete a task or solve a problem. Creativity is an essential ingredient.

Initiative. An entrepreneur must have initiative, accepting personal responsibility for actions, and above all make good use of resources.

Goal setter. An entrepreneur must be able to set challenging but realistic goals.

Moderate risk taker. An entrepreneur must be a moderate risk taker and learn from any failures.

Rarely does an entrepreneur have total strengths in each of these areas. The underlying key questions are: Can the entrepreneur bring together a team that will complement each other with varying types of skills (marketing operations, production, financial management, general management, personnel, legal, tax)? Can these individuals be molded into an effective workforce with common objectives?

Summary

Since the early 1960s the venture capital industry has established an enviable record of performance. The dollars and guidance of the venture capitalist has been combined with the knowledge and drive of the entrepreneur to create jobs, spur innovation, increase productivity, and multiply profits. The venture capital industry has established and attracted a management cadre of highly professional and highly motivated professionals with the expertise to assist the small business community of the United States.

The entrepreneurial spirit is being revived in the United States. A search and quest for a better way of life, for creating a meaningful estate, for the excitement that is inherent in giving birth to a new idea or a new company, coupled with the inherent risk of any new venture, is a strong motivational urge being felt by many individuals.

During these times of intense economic pressure, small business must be given the opportunity to continue to be a great source of growth and opportunity for any economic renaissance to take place in an area. This opportunity is supported by the dollars and guidance of the venture capitalists in that area.

6
Entrepreneurs, Angels, and Economic Renaissance

William E. Wetzel, Jr.

The strength of the U.S. economy increasingly depends on the vitality of entrepreneurial ventures. The comparative advantages of the United States within the world economy and of individual regions within the United States spring from a supply of entrepreneurial resources—both tangible and intangible. A spirit of ingenuity and self-reliance, a large and growing pool of technological know-how, a supply of risk capital, both formal and informal, and a skilled labor force have permitted the United States to excel in the development of new products and processes and in the formation of innovative companies.

As innovative processes become routine, competitive advantages shift toward countries, regions, and firms with the most efficient production functions—the lowest labor, energy, raw material, and transportation costs. These resources tend to be more abundant in developing countries than in the United States, and within the United States more abundant in some regions than in others. Thus, it is critical that the United States and regions within the United States maintain the ability to spawn innovative firms and to develop new ideas and products. Implications for the economic renaissance of many regions involve a strategic emphasis on entrepreneurs, innovation, and the capital required to create new ventures.

One need not look far for reasons to build a region's economic renaissance on an entrepreneurial strategy. For example, between 1958 and 1977—a period of expansion for all major industries—the number of jobs in small business–dominated industries grew faster than in industries dominated by large firms.[1] From November of 1982 to October of 1984 small business–dominated industries added jobs at a rate over twice that of industries dominated by large firms: 11.4

percent compared to 5.3 percent.[2] In 1981 and 1982, small, independent firms created over 2.6 million new jobs, more than compensating for the 1.6 million jobs lost by large industries.[3] David Birch of MIT found that firms employing twenty or fewer employees generated 66 percent of all new jobs between 1969 and 1976. For the Northeast region, all net new jobs were generated by small business.[4]

Despite the evidence supporting an entrepreneurial approach to economic development, the implications for policy initiatives designed to implement such a strategy are far from clear. Birch summarized his data as follows:

> A pattern begins to emerge in all of this. The job generating firm tends to be small. It tends to be dynamic (or unstable, depending on your viewpoint)—the kind of firm banks feel very uncomfortable about. It tends to be young. In short, the firms that can and do generate the most jobs are the ones that are the most difficult to reach through conventional policy initiatives.[5]

Birch observed in his conclusion:

> It is not clear what to offer job-replacing firms. Some have argued persuasively that small businesses need, use well, and cannot easily get, capital. Beyond that, however, the answers are less clear.[6]

Risk Capital Markets

Creative ideas, managers with entrepreneurial tendencies, and risk capital are the raw materials from which new ventures are constructed and old ventures are adapted to changing markets. Of these essential ingredients, risk capital is often the most elusive.

Any useful discussion of the availability of risk capital must first recognize the diverse nature of the commodity and its sources of supply. The market for risk capital consists of at least three segments, each with a unique set of distinguishing characteristics: (1) the public equity market; (2) the professional venture capital market; and (3) the market for informal risk capital (business angels).

Although the boundaries separating these segments are indistinct and often overlap, an appreciation of the distinctions is essential for entrepreneurs seeking funds and for economic development strategies designed to influence the availability of risk capital.

The public equity market and the professional venture capital market are relatively efficient and well understood. At the risk of oversimplification, it can be said that if an entrepreneur is trying to raise from $2 million to $5 million (or more) for an appealing venture, the speculative new issues market represents a potential source of funds.

The professional venture capitalist is generally interested in ventures that require $500,000 (or more) of poststart-up financing, are likely to generate sales in excess of $20 million within five to seven years, and expect to go public or sell out by that time. A recent survey of the largest and most active professional venture capital firms found that the range of an individual investment was from $300,000 to $4 million and the size of a typical individual investment was $813,000. The figures were similar for SBICs, but substantially higher for corporate venture affiliates.[7]

The informal risk capital market, on the other hand, is virtually invisible, inefficient, and often misunderstood. Yet searching for an angel is appropriate for a technology-based inventor looking for development funds or an entrepreneur looking for less than $500,000 to start or expand a venture. Inefficiency and the invisible nature of the angel segment of the capital markets contribute to perceptions that funds for such purposes are unavailable.

Entrepreneurs starting ventures with potential revenues of $2 million to $20 million in five years (and employment potential from twenty to five hundred) typically require less than $1 million to get started and their companies are likely to remain privately held. Once personal funds and other friendly sources are exhausted (often somewhere in the $50,000 range), these entrepreneurs have no institutional sources of equity capital to which they can turn. Faced with this gap in the institutional risk capital market, many entrepreneurs turn to individual investors (business angels) for financing. Venture investing in amounts between $50,000 and $500,000 is the domain of angels. But they are tough to find!

There is evidence to suggest that individual investors (despite their low profile) represent the largest pool of risk capital in the United States. Although there are no data documenting the total financing provided by individuals, clues can be found. For example, in 1981, private placements reported by corporations to the SEC under Rule 146 totaled over $1 billion. In a 1980 SEC survey of a sample of issuers who filed Form 146, it was found that corporate issuers were engaged primarily in high technology or in other manufacturing or nonfinancial services and that these companies generally were young and employing few workers. The survey disclosed that 87 percent of those buying corporate issues were individual investors or personal trusts. The average amount invested by an individual in a corporate issue was $74,000.[8] Note that Rule 146 data exclude financings exempt from registration because of their intrastate nature (Rule 147) and financing by closely held firms under small-offering exemptions (Rules 240 and 242).

Regulation D was developed by the SEC in response to the Small Business Investment Incentive Act of 1980 and became effective on April 15, 1982. Regulation D exempts certain private and limited offerings from the registration requirements of the Securities Act of 1933 and replaced Rules 240, 242, and 146. Issuers claiming an exemption under Regulation D in its first year offered an estimated $15.5 billion of securities in over 7,200 filings. Corporations accounted for 43 percent of the value ($6.7 billion) and 32 percent of the offerings (2,304). Under Rule 504 (limited offerings under $500,000), corporations raised $220 million, an average of $200,000 per firm and a median of $150,000. The typical corporate issuer tended to be small, with five or fewer employees (60.7 percent) and an operating history of two years or less (68.8 percent). The typical corporate issuer had less than ten stockholders (64.3 percent), revenues and assets of $500,000 or less (75.5 percent and 71.3 percent respectively), and stockholders equity of $50,000 or less (87.9 percent). Seventy-seven percent were not operating at a profit.[9]

Other empirical data confirm the importance of angels in the financing of entrepreneurial ventures. In an examination of capital market imperfections, Charles River Associates (CRA) studied the composition of external funds raised by small, technology-based firms prior to making initial public offerings. The study revealed that between 1970 and 1974 "unaffiliated individuals" accounted for 15 percent of external funds, whereas venture capitalists accounted for 12 percent. When the data were classified by stage (age of venture), unaffiliated individuals provided 17 percent of external capital during the start-up year, whereas venture capitalists provided 11 percent.

CRA excluded from their examination of capital market imperfections the market in which firms raise funds from "individuals who act informally as providers of venture funds." Yet CRA commented that "they may represent the largest source of venture capital in the country."[10]

Similar patterns can be found in David Brophy's study of financial support for new, technology-based firms that were incorporated and operating from 1965 to 1970. In a sample of Boston-area firms, private individuals (excluding founders, friends, and relatives) provided 14 percent of total financing and SBICs and private venture capital firms provided 15 percent. The figures for a sample of Ann Arbor and Detroit firms were 16 percent from individuals and 2 percent from venture capitalists.[11]

Clearly, angels play a key role in the financing of entrepreneurial ventures. One or more wealthy believers often provide seed capital, help solve problems, and exploit the opportunities associated with commercializing an invention or innovation or with starting a new enterprise. Most entrepreneurs have heard of business angels. Some entrepreneurs have found them. However, no one has really discovered where angels come from, how many there are, how to find them, or what angels look for in a venture proposal.

Informal Risk Capital Research

The majority of risk capital research has been devoted to studies of the institutional risk capital markets. The limited body of informal risk capital research has been linked by a number of more or less common lines of inquiry. These issues should be of interest to economic development officials. The issues that link informal risk capital research include the following questions:

1. What is the scale of informal risk capital investing in numbers of transactions, numbers of investors, and dollars invested?

2. What are the channels of communication that link entrepreneurs with informal investors and informal investors with each other?

3. Are there regional differences in the absolute and/or effective availability of informal risk capital?

4. What are the characteristics of the screening and evaluation

models employed by informal investors? How diverse are informal investor decision models? Do they differ from the models employed by professional venture capitalists?

5. Does informal risk capital complement or compete with institutional venture capital? Are there circumstances under which it is more appropriate for an entrepreneur to seek funds from an angel than from a professional venture capital firm?

6. Is informal risk capital more or less expensive than professional venture capital?

7. Are there subsets of informal investors that tend to behave differently, for example, active vs. passive investors, more affluent vs. less affluent investors, self-made investors vs. those with inherited wealth?

8. Are informal investors motivated exclusively by monetary rewards or do they sometimes seek nonfinancial returns? What are these nonfinancial considerations and how powerful are they?

During 1979 and 1980, with funding from the Office of Advocacy of the U.S. Small Business Administration, Seymour and Wetzel attempted to answer some of these questions.[12] Data were collected from 133 individual investors in New England. The research focused on the role of informal investors as a source of funds for three types of investment situations:

1. Financing for technology-based investors.
2. Start-up and early-stage financing for emerging firms.
3. Equity financing for small, established firms growing faster than internal cash flows can support.

The three areas addressed represent situations that seldom attract financing from institutional venture capital sources.

Investment Record

The sample of New England angels reported risk capital investments totaling over $16 million in 320 ventures between 1976 and 1980, an average of one deal every two years for each investor. The average size of their investments was $50,000, and the median size was $20,000. Thirty-six percent of their investments involved less than $10,000, whereas 24 percent involved over $50,000. In 60 percent of their transactions these investors participated with other investors. Participation with other investors permits venture financing that approaches the $500,000 interest threshold of institutional venture investors.

Venture Life Cycle Preference

Forty percent of past financings were start-ups, and 80 percent involved ventures less than five years old. Sixty-three percent of their investments were in companies that had not achieved break-even operations (another definition of start-up). With respect to future investments, 78 percent reported a strong interest in start-up and early-stage financing for emerging firms. One-third of the sample expressed a strong interest in prestart-up financing for technology-based inventors. The principal investment criterion cited by investors interested in inventors was that the technology be in a field that they understood and could evaluate for themselves. The following comments illustrate this overriding consideration: "a field in which I have some technical competence"; "fields in which I am sufficiently experienced to permit evaluation"; "related to my background in organic chemistry and pharmaceuticals"; "those I know: electronics, physics, mechanics"; and "it is limited to what I know and understand myself, especially about the marketplace, or can get trustworthy opinions on."

Venture Relationships

The angels in the New England sample were well educated and had experience in the management of start-up ventures. Ninety-five percent held four-year college degrees and 51 percent had graduate degrees. Of the graduate degrees, 44 percent were in a technical field and 33 percent in business or economics (generally an M.B.A.). Seventy-five percent had been involved in the start-up of a new venture. Eighty-four percent reported that they expect to play an active role with the ventures they finance, typically an informal consulting role or service on a working board of directors.

Geographic Patterns

The tendency of informal investors to maintain close working contact with ventures they finance is reflected in the geographic distribution of their portfolios. Three-quarters of the firms financed by these investors were within 300 miles of the investor (roughly one day's drive) and 58 percent were within 50 miles. The tendency of informal investors to invest close to home also reflects the absence of systematic channels of communication between investors and entrepreneurs. The likelihood of an investment opportunity coming to an individual investor's attention increases, probably exponentially, the shorter the distance between the two parties.

Industry Preferences

Although the interests of the New England investors covered the entire spectrum of business and industry categories, there was a clear preference for manufacturing enterprises in general and for high-technology manufacturing in particular. Sixty-four percent expressed a strong interest in high technology manufacturing, 33 percent in industrial product manufacturing, and 30 percent in service firms. Only 5 percent expressed a strong interest in wholsale trade, 3 percent in retail trade, and 1 percent in transportation firms.

Exit Expectations

Risk capital is *patient money*. The patience level of informal investors was tested in terms of expected holding periods. The median expected holding period was five to seven years. However, 24 percent either considered the holding period unimportant or expected to hold their risk capital investments longer than ten years, a patience level well in excess of the exit expectations of institutional venture capitalists. Forty-seven percent of the investors reported that provisions for liquidating their investment were definitely or generally included in their initial investment agreement.

Rejected Proposals

The typical angel seriously considers and then rejects two or three investment opportunities annually. The most common reasons cited for rejection were lack of confidence in management, unsatisfactory risk–reward ratios, absence of a well-defined business plan, the investor's unfamiliarity with products, processes, or markets, or the venture was a business the investor "did not want to be in." The following comments reflect the range of reasons for rejecting investment proposals: "Risk–return ratio was not adequate"; "In most cases management did not seem adequate to the task at hand"; "Simply not interested in the proposed businesses. Saw no socioeconomic value in them"; "Unable to agree on price"; "Too much wishful thinking"; "One of two key principals not sufficiently committed—too involved with another activity"; "Unfamiliar with business"; and "Wife refused."

Risk–Reward Relationships

Investors perceive significant differences between the risks associated with investing in early-stage situations and those associated with later-stage financing. Median expectations of losses exceeding 50 percent of their investment were anticipated for investments in seven out of ten inventors, six out of ten start-ups, five out of ten firms under one year old, four out of ten firms under five years old, and two out of ten established firms.

Reward expectations for successful investments reflected the perceived risk of losses. With respect to successful investments, investors anticipated median five-year capital gains of ten times for inventors and start-ups, six times for firms under one year old, five times for firms under five years old, and three times for established firms. Median portfolio expectations were a consistent 20 percent per year for all types of portfolios (inventors, start-ups, and so forth) except for portfolios of investments in established firms where the median expectation was 15 percent per year.

Although risk capital is clearly expensive, and deserves to be, the reward expectations of informal investors seem low when compared to the range of expectations usually attributed to professional venture capital firms. The relatively low cost of informal risk capital may be due in part to the nonfinancial rewards that often motivate individual investors.

Nonfinancial Rewards

As distinguished from professional venture capitalists, informal investors frequently look for nonfinancial returns from their risk capital portfolios. These nonfinancial returns fall into several categories. Some reflect a sense of social responsibility and some reflect forms of psychological income (or so-called hot buttons) that motivate individuals. The list of nonfinancial considerations includes creating jobs in areas of high unemployment, ventures developing socially useful technology (for example, medical or energy-saving technology), ventures contributing to urban revitalization, ventures created by female or minority entrepreneurs, and the personal satisfaction derived from assisting entrepreneurs build successful ventures.

A significant fraction of the sampled investors reported that they would accept a lower return (or undertake a higher risk) in situations providing some form of nonfinancial reward. Forty-five percent of the sample considered assisting entrepreneurs a form of nonfinancial reward. Between 35 and 40 percent reported that they would accept lower returns when their investment helped create employment in their communities or contributed to the development of socially useful technology. Median rate of return reductions of 20 percent were associated with investments that create employment and that assist minority entrepreneurs.

Public Policy and Market Efficiency

Despite the critical role played by individual investors in the financing of many entrepreneurial ventures, there is a continuing perception that gaps exist in the capital markets for smaller firms. This perception raises questions about the outlook for an economic renaissance based on the promotion of entrepreneurship. Though such gaps have not been documented convincingly, the capital gap folklore maintains that there are shortages of product development financing for technology-based inventors, of start-up financing for ventures that fail to meet the criteria of professional venture capital investors, and of equity financing for closely held firms that are growing at a faster rate than internal cash flows can support. For evidence supporting the folklore, see the study of high-growth firms in New Hampshire by Wetzel and Wilson.[13] The SBIC program, created by Congress in 1958, was an attempt to fill such gaps. Following the 1980 White House Conference on Small Business, efforts to deal with the gap led to the Small Business Investment Incentive Act of 1980 and the SEC's new Regulation D streamlining securities law for small business.

The capital gap folklore is based on the observable behavior of financial institutions, including equity-oriented SBICs and professional venture capital firms. However, capital gaps may be more apparent than real. The folklore overlooks the investment record of informal risk capital investors—business angels. (Angels do not include founders, friends, or relatives.) Not only do these angels exist, they appear to represent the largest pool of risk capital in the country, and they tend to invest in precisely those areas cited as gaps in the capital markets for entrepreneurs.

Capital gaps can be created indirectly when markets fail to function efficiently. Modern financial theory rests on efficient capital market assumptions. Information about sources of funds and investment opportunities is presumed to be readily available to buyers and sellers of capital. This necessary condition is far from fulfilled in the angel segment of the risk capital market. In the absence of efficient markets, the flow of capital from less productive to more productive uses will be impeded. The efficiency issue is a cause for concern because angels play an essential role in the financing of entrepreneurs.

Data describing the channels through which information about opportunities for investment in entrepreneurial ventures is transmitted can be found in the work of Hoffman[14] and Seymour and Wetzel.[15] Both studies reveal the significance of an informal network of friends and business associates in the referral process. In the Seymour and Wetzel study, informal investors were provided with a list of sources of investment opportunities and asked to classify each as a "frequent source," "occasional source," or "not a source" of investment proposals they had seriously considered during the previous five years. Table 6–1 displays the distribution of responses.

The Seymour and Wetzel study tested informal investors' perception of the effectiveness of existing channels of communication between bonafide entrepreneurs seeking risk capital and investors like themselves. "Totally dissatisfied" respondents outnumbered "definitely satisfied" respondents by over four-to-one.

Seymour and Wetzel also tested the interest of informal investors in a confidential referral service that would direct investment oppor-

Table 6–1
Referral Sources

	Frequency of Classification		
	Frequent Source	*Occasional Source*	*Not a Source*
Business associates	62	37	18
Friends	59	44	15
Active personal search	46	29	36
Investment bankers	17	28	66
Business brokers	12	36	62
Commercial bankers	9	30	68
Other	7	5	46
Attorneys	3	50	55
Accountants	2	41	66

tunities to their attention. Thirty-eight percent of the sample reported a moderate interest and 50 percent reported a strong interest in such a service.[16]

These results add emphasis to an issue raised by Charles River Associates in their 1976 analysis of capital market imperfections:

> It is not clear whether the existing system for generating and disseminating information about investment opportunities is efficient. In other words, it is not clear whether it could be improved in a cost-effective manner.[17]

In view of the significance of informal investors as a source of seed capital for entrepreneurs, the efficiency of the communication networks linking individual investors with each other and with investment opportunities is a matter of considerable interest to investors, entrepreneurs, and economic development officials. Economic development officials should also be concerned because of the potential impact of the so-called discouragement effect on entrepreneurs.

> Analagous to the discouragement effect in labor markets that lowers the official number of job seekers, there is undoubtedly a similar discouragement effect operating among unsuccessful seekers of venture capital, would-be seekers of venture capital, and would-be entrepreneurs.[18]

For entrepreneurs prematurely abandoning the search for funds, the effective cost of risk capital is infinite, and society bears the cost of lost opportunities to establish new ventures or expand old ones. By providing more efficient methods for raising seed capital, public policy may be able to overcome some of the social costs associated with inefficient markets and the discouragement effect.

Public Policy and External Economies

An activity for which the social rate of return exceeds the private rate of return is said to generate external economies—public benefits that cannot be captured by private investors. The entrepreneurial process, of which venture investing is a part, is generally believed to generate significant external or social benefits. This conclusion has been substantiated with respect to the innovative capability of entrepreneurs. In a sample of seventeen industrial innovations, a prominent economist estimated the median private rate of return at 25 percent and the median social rate of return at 56 percent.[19]

In the presence of external benefits, the allocation of private funds to entrepreneurial ventures, including generating information about investment opportunities, will fall short of a socially optimal allocation, even if there are no imperfections in the capital markets.

> To the extent that investment in small, technology-based firms produces external economies, too few resources will be allocated to all phases of investing in them, including generating information about investment opportunities.[20]

Public benefits resulting from an enhanced flow of jobs, innovative technology, and tax revenues from entrepreneurial ventures provide a rationale for public support of efforts to improve the efficiency of the risk capital markets.

Playing with Numbers

Playing with Numbers is a flight of fancy designed to locate the outer limits of the invisible informal risk capital market. In a sense, the discussion puts some boundaries on our ignorance. The numbers are crude. They are intended to provide a sense of perspective and to whet the appetites of economic development officials and those interested in risk capital research. The analysis, however crude, points out the considerable potential for risk capital financing by individuals with sufficent knowledge and experience in business and financial matters to evaluate the risks and rewards of investing in entrepreneurs.

1. The number of corporations in the United States exceeds two million. Of the total corporate population, only one in one hundred (twenty thousand) is publicly traded, only one in two hundred (ten thousand) has enough stockholders to be required to report regularly to the SEC, and the shares of only one in four hundred (five thousand) are listed on an organized exchange. In other words, 99 percent of U.S. corporations are privately held.

    Approximately five hundred firms enter the public equity market annually. Over the last fifteen years the number of initial public offerings has ranged from less than fifty to over one thousand. In view of infant mortality rates, it is not unreasonable to assume that well under 1 percent of corporate start-ups will both survive and ultimately develop a public market for their shares.

2. The number of firms financed by institutional venture capitalists (including equity-oriented SBICs) is in the neighborhood of two thousand per year. Less than half are start-ups. The prospect of a public offering or merger with a larger firm within five to seven years is a necessary condition to attracting institutional venture capital.

3. The number of business start-ups exceeds five hundred thousand per year. If 95 percent of these start-ups are too small to require outside equity financing, there are still twenty-five thousand start-ups that need outside capital and apparently succeed in raising it. To carry this flight of fancy one step further, if these start-ups raise an average of $200,000 apiece, the aggregate outside equity funding for these ventures totals $5 billion annually.

Question: If institutional venture capitalists finance less than one thousand start-ups annually, where do the other twenty-four thousand (or whatever figure you prefer) find their equity capital? *Answer:*

Probably from informal investors—business angels. The figures suggest that informal investors finance as many as twenty times the number of firms financed by institutional venture capitalists or by the public equity markets.

Similar conclusions can be reached by playing with the numbers of potential business angels.

1. The "Forbes Four Hundred Richest People in America" represent a combined net worth of $134 billion, an average of $335 million each.[21] Forty percent (165) of the Four Hundred built their fortunes without any significant inheritance. The combined net worth of these self-made millionaires is over $50 billion. If 10 percent of their net worth is available for venture-type investing, the pool of funds available from these 165 individuals alone is $5 billion. In addition to their role as potential angels, the very wealthy also are significant investors in professional venture capital firms.

2. There are over five hundred thousand individuals in the United States with a net worth in excess of $1 million ("accredited investors" by one of the SEC's Regulation D criteria). If 40 percent of these potential angels also are self-made and presumably interested in backing entrepreneurs, then the angel pool numbers about two hundred thousand. If half of these angels invest in any given year and ante up $50,000 apiece, that puts the total number of active angels at one hundred thousand annually and the amount invested at $5 billion. If the typical deal involves four angels co-venturing, then the number of ventures financed is on the order of twenty-five thousand, each receiving an average of $200,000. It is no accident that these figures conveniently conform to the estimates of the number of ventures financed by informal investors.

The extent of our ignorance is measured by the fact that we know very little about the ventures, the investors, or the processes involved in the funding of approximately twenty-five thousand firms and approximately $5 billion of informal risk capital investing per year. Perhaps of greater significance, we know nothing at all about the cost to society of opportunities to launch successful entrepreneurial ventures that were lost because efforts to raise risk capital were unsuccessful.

Venture Capital Network, Inc.

Venture Capital Network, Inc. (VCN) is an experiment in expediting the financing of entrepreneurs by individual investors (business angels). VCN is the product of twelve months of deliberations by the Economic Long Range Planning Committee of the Business and Industry Association of New Hampshire (BIA). New Hampshire competes with other New England states, not only to attract existing business and industry but also to provide assistance to entrepreneurs starting new companies.

The committee evaluated programs in neighboring states that provide debt and equity financing for entrepreneurial ventures and appraised the impact of similar programs on New Hampshire's fiscal resources. They concluded that the most effective step that the BIA and the business community could take to match the financial capabilities of neighboring states would be to create a private sector program to enhance the information networks that link entrepreneurs with investors and that link investors with each. A proposal to establish VCN was approved by BIA's Board of Directors on July 14, 1983.

VCN is designed to overcome inefficiencies in the informal risk capital market by performing the following four functions:

1. Identifying opportunities for risk capital investment in entrepreneurial ventures and profiling their investment characteristics.
2. Identifying active informal investors and profiling their investment objectives.
3. Providing a timely, confidential, and objective referral mechanism serving both entrepreneurs and investors.
4. Enhancing the communications networks that link informal investors with each other and enhancing the flow of information through those networks.

VCN is designed to minimize the cost of an entrepreneur's search for capital and to provide informal investors with a convenient system for examining investment opportunities that meet their screening criteria. Although primarily intended to serve New England entrepreneurs, and thereby New Hampshire's economy, VCN has imposed no geographic limitations on the scope of its services.

Corporate Status

VCN was incorporated in September of 1983 as a not-for-profit affiliate of the BIA and established a contractual relationship with the Office of Small Business Programs of the University of New Hampshire for the management of the program. VCN is accountable to a seven-member board of directors, five of whom are nominated by the BIA and two by the university's Office of Small Business Programs. VCN itself has no staff and no assets other than ownership of the investor and entrepreneur data bases.

Securities and Exchange Commission

VCN has received "no action" letters from the SEC permitting it to operate without registering as a broker–dealer under Section 15(a) of the Securities Exchange Act of 1934 or as an investment advisor under Section 203 of the Investment Advisors Act of 1940. VCN conducts no independent investigations to verify the factual information submitted by entrepreneurs and investors and makes no representations or warranties regarding the accuracy or completeness of the information provided by entrepreneurs and investors. It solicits no character or credit references from entrepreneurs or prospective investors and does not evaluate or endorse the merits of investment opportunities presented through its services. Investment transactions resulting from VCN introductions are on a negotiated basis between entrepreneurs and investors, without any participation by or remuneration to VCN.

A series of disclaimers to investors and entrepreneurs, prepared by VCN's legal counsel, are prominently displayed in all VCN application materials. The disclaimers serve to define the functions VCN will and will not perform. In view of the fact that investments resulting from introductions by VCN may involve a high degree of risk, VCN requires investors to certify that they qualify as "accredited investors" as defined in Rule 501(a) of Regulation D or that they "possess such knowledge and experience in financial and business matters that they are capable of evaluating the merits and risks or prospective investments."

Operating Procedures

VCN's referral mechanism is triggered by inquiries from either investors or entrepreneurs. A two-stage referral process is employed. Entrepreneurs applying to VCN submit a profile of their investment proposal together with a two-page Executive Summary of their business plan. Using a computer data base management system, VCN screens the investor data base to identify potential sources of financing. VCN also retains the investment opportunity profile in the entrepreneur data base for access by future investors registering with VCN.

Potential investors identified by the screening process receive a blind copy of the entrepreneur's investment opportunity profile and respond positively or negatively to the opportunity. In the case of negative responses, investors report the reasons for their lack of interest. The reasons for negative responses are provided to the entrepreneur and are evaluated by VCN as a means of refining the profiling and referral process. In the case of positive responses, investors are provided with a blind copy of the Executive Summary of the entrepreneur's business plan, and again respond positively or negatively. Reasons for negative responses at this second stage are also provided to entrepreneurs and evaluated by VCN. In the case of positive responses, VCN introduces the investors and entrepreneurs involved. VCN withdraws from participation at the conclusion of introductions.

In the case of investor applicants, VCN screens the entrepreneur data base for appropriate investment opportunities. Potential opportunities are referred using the methodology outlined above. The investor's profile is retained in the investor data base for access by future entrepreneurs registering with VCN. Both investor and investment opportunity profiles are updated on a periodic basis

Operating Performance

From the inception of operations in July of 1984 through October of 1985, VCN enrolled over three hundred investors and over one hundred and thirty entrepreneurs. Twelve thousand Stage I matches have been generated, 2,500 Stage II matches, and 765 investor–entrepreneur introductions initiated. Through VCN's services, participating entrepreneurs have been introduced to an average of 5.75 investors. Participating investors have asked to meet an average of 2.5 entrepreneurs. Since VCN does not become involved in investment negotiations, it has no systemmatic method for tracking the outcome of introductions. Collection of these data are undertaken periodically as an independent research effort.

At least five ventures are known to have been funded by VCN investors. One small, high-technology firm attracted a low six figure investment from a VCN investor. Another venture raised a five figure sum, and a third firm raised funds aggregated in low six figures from four investors introduced by VCN. The president of the third firm was quoted in the *Wall Street Journal:* "VCN is extremeley useful to a company like ours. These investors wouldn't have found us any other way."

Future Plans

It seems clear that VCN is performing a useful function in the angel segment of the risk capital markets. The scale of VCN's activities is expected to expand significantly in the years ahead, enhanced in part by the support of a group of professional sponsors. VCN sponsors currently include the Shawmut Bank of Boston, Deloitte Haskins and Sells, and Peat, Marwick, Mitchell & Co.

VCN is also exploring cooperative arrangements with other not-for-profit organizations, including, for example, Science Park Development Corp. (SPDC) SPDC is a joint venture involving Yale University, the Olin Corporation, the City of New Haven, and the State of Connecticut. SPDC's projects include an incubator facility housing over eighty technology-based, start-up ventures. A number of these developing ventures are expected to benefit from angel-type financing.

VCN is assisting not-for-profit organizations in the creation of VCN counterparts in regions outside New England. The first VCN offspring has been established in Tulsa, Oklahoma, and is managed by the University of Tulsa. VCN has also been asked by the Ministry of Trade and Industry of the Republic of the Philippines to assist in creating a Philippine counterpart of VCN as part of their Small and Medium Enterprise Development Program.

Conclusion

A multitude of factors will affect the success of an economic renaissance built on an entrepreneurial strategy. Regions that have successfully developed an entrepreneurial economic base have done so over a period of years, even generations. In the past, the process has worked its will without benefit of public policy designed to promote entrepreneurship. Entrepreneurs, not unlike wildflowers, appear to spring up of their own accord when conditions are right. Like wildflowers, they are difficult to propagate or transplant. Predicting which ventures will thrive in any given location is a talent yet to be demonstrated by public officials. It seems unlikely that an economic renaissance will be successful if it attempts to target particular markets, industries, or firms for the promotion of entrepreneurship.

To carry the wildflower analogy one step further, it appears that entrepreneurs can be served best by simply improving the entrepreneurial climate and by creating a breeze that will blow the entrepreneurial pollen around more broadly. A variety of regional programs can be designed to enhance the entrepreneurial climate and that leave to entrepreneurs and the marketplace the determination of which ventures will sprout, survive, and grow.

The entrepreneurial climate includes a host of economic, political, and sociological factors. In part, the climate is measured by the efficiency of the markets entrepreneurs turn to for resources: people, capital, materials, and know-how. In the capital markets, the informal risk capital segment is the least efficient. It is composed of a diverse and dispersed population of individuals of means. Research data and the experience of VCN suggest that the efficiency of the informal risk capital market can be improved dramatically. Regional mechanisms for the dissemination of information about resources of informal risk capital (angel money) and about opportunities to invest in entrepreneurial ventures have proven effective in enhancing the entrepreneurial climate.

Notes

1. *The State of Small Business: A Report of the President* (Washington, D.C.: Government Printing Office, 1984), XV.
2. *The State of Small Business: A Report of the President* (Washington, D.C.: Government Printing Office, 1985), XI.
3. *State of Small Business*, 1984, XV.
4. D. L. Birch, *The Job Generation Process* (Washington, D.C.: MIT Program on Neighborhood and Regional Change, Economic Development Administration, U.S. Department of Commerce, 1979), 8.
5. Ibid., 17.

6. Ibid., 21.

7. D. E. Gumpert and J. A. Timmons, "Disregard Many Old Myths about Getting Venture Capital," *Harvard Business Review* (January–February 1982): 156.

8. *Report of the Use of the Rule 146 Exemption in Capital Formation* (Washington, D.C.: Directorate of Economic and Policy Analysis, U.S. Securities and Exchange Commission, 1983), 15.

9. *An Analysis of Regulation D* (Washington, D.C.: Directorate of Economic and Policy Analysis, U.S. Securities and Exchange Commission, 1984), 1.

10. Charles River Associates, Inc., *An Analysis of Capital Market Imperfections* (Washington, D.C.: Experimental Technology Incentives Program, National Bureau of Standards, 1976), 74.

11. D. T. Brophy, "Venture Capital Research," in *Encyclopedia of Entrepreneurship* (Englewood Cliffs, N.J.: Prentice-Hall, 1982), 176.

12. C. R. Seymour and W. E. Wetzel, *Informal Risk Capital in New England* (Durham, N.H.: University of New Hampshire, 1981), 1–64.

13. W. E. Wetzel and I. G. Wilson, "Seed Capital Gaps: Evidence from High-Growth Ventures" (Paper delivered at the Entrepreneurship Research Conference, The Wharton School, University of Pennsylvania, Philadelphia, 17–19 April 1985), 1–20.

14. C. A. Hoffman, "The Venture Capital Investment Process: A Particular Aspect of Regional Economic Development" (Ph.D. Diss., University of Texas at Austin, 1972).

15. Seymour and Wetzel, *Informal Risk Capital in New England, 1–64.*

16. Ibid., 59.

17. Charles River Associates, *Analysis of Capital Market Imperfections,* 151.

18. M. G. Boyland, "What We Know and Don't Know about Venture Capital," (Paper delivered at the Annual Meeting of the American Economic Association, Chicago, Ill., December 1981), 1–18.

19. E. Mansfield, "Entrepreneurship and the Management of Innovation," in *Entrepreneurship and the Outlook for America,* ed. J. Bachman (New York: The Free Press, 1983), 103.

20. Charles River Associates, *Analysis of Capital Market Imperfections,* 152.

21. "The Four Hundred Richest People in America," *The Forbes Four Hundred,* October 28, 1985.

About the Contributors

Barry M. Davis has over twenty years of experience in venture capital investment and building and creating new and emerging growth companies. He is currently President and Chief Executive Officer of Alliance Business Investment Company. He also serves as the Managing General Partner of Davis Venture Partners (DVP), a $30 million venture capital limited partnership, which will focus its investment strategy on investments in Oklahoma, Texas, and the surrounding southwestern states. Mr. Davis is also a partner in the Davis companies—energy/natural resources and real estate development groups with primary activities in the Southwest. He also serves on the Board of Directors of a number of corporations, including Allco Chemical Corporation; Advanced Manufacturing Systems, Inc.; Energy Minerals, Inc.; and Apple Investments, Inc. In 1980, Mr. Davis was elected National Chairman of the Board of Governors of NASBIC, a venture capital industry trade association, and he has also served as President of the organization's Southwest Regional Association. In 1975, he received the National Achievement Award in the venture capital industry for his efforts in founding NASBIC's Venture Capital Management Institute, the formal training ground for a significant portion of the venture capital managers in the United States.

William A. Sahlman is an Associate Professor of Finance at Harvard Business School. He received an A.B. degree in Economics from Princeton University, an M.B.A. from Harvard University, and a Ph.D. in Business Economics, also from Harvard. He has developed a new second-year course entitled "Entrepreneurial Finance." Dr. Sahlman's research focuses on the investment and financing decisions made in entrepreneurial ventures. Dr. Sahlman's most recent article, "Capital

Market Myopia" (coauthored with Howard H. Stevenson), was published in the initial volume of the *Journal of Business Venturing* (Winter 1985). The article assessed the role of the financial markets in supplying funds to the Winchester disk drive industry from 1977 to 1984. Dr. Sahlman is a member of the Board of Directors of the Butcher Polish Company, Business Research Corporation, First Call Corporation, and American Management Company. He is an advisor to Nathan/Tyler Productions, creators of *In Search of Excellence—The Film*. He has recently become a member of the Executive Committee of the Securities and Exchange Commission's Office of Small Business Policy.

Donald L. Sexton is Director of the Center for Entrepreneurship and holder of the Caruth Chair of Entrepreneurship at Baylor University. A native of Ohio, Dr. Sexton was formerly an Associate Professor of Business Administration in the Graduate Business Administration Program at Sangamon State University. Dr. Sexton worked in business for fifteen years prior to joining the academic community. His last eight years in industry were at executive-level positions. He was known as a "turnaround" specialist, having successfully managed four firms from losses to profitable operations. He continues to maintain contact with businesses through his activities at the center, consulting, and membership on four Boards of Directors. He received his bachelor's degree in Mathematics from Wilmington College and his M.B.A. and Ph.D. from The Ohio State University. Dr. Sexton has been active in the Academy of Management, the International Council for Small Business, and the International Symposium for Small Business. He has served on the editorial review boards of the *Journal of Small Business Management, Journal of Venturing,* and *Academy of Management Review*. He has written and presented numerous papers on various aspects of small business and entrepreneurship, is a frequent speaker on the topic, and has published three text books: *Encyclopedia of Entrepreneurship,* with Calvin Kent and Karl Vesper; *Experiences in Entrepreneurship and Small Business Management,* with Phil Van Auken; and *Starting and Operating a Business in Texas,* coauthored with Michael Jenkins.

Raymond W. Smilor is the Associate Director of the IC² Institute, the University of Texas at Austin, and serves there as a member of the faculty in the Department of Marketing in the College of Business Administration. He holds the Judson Neff Centennial Fellowship in the IC² Institute. He is also the Director and Editor-in-Chief of the *Journal of High Technology Marketing*. He has served as a research fellow for a National Science Foundation international exchange program on computers and management between the United States and the Soviet Union. He is co-editor of four books: *Corporate Creativity: Robust Companies and the Entrepreneurial Spirit* (Praeger, 1984); *Improving U.S. Energy Security* (Ballinger, 1985); *Managing Take-Off in Fast Growth Companies* (Praeger, 1986); *The Art and Science of Entrepreneurship* (Ballinger, 1986). He is also coauthor of two books: *Financing and Managing Fast-Growth Companies: The Venture Capital Process* (Lexington Books, 1985) and *The New-Business Incubator: Linking Talent, Technology, Capital, and Know-How* (Lexington Books, forthcoming). He serves as a consultant to business, government, and the nonprofit sector. He is President of the Management Strategies Group and a Director of the Texas LYCEUM Association.

Howard H. Stevenson is the Sarofim–Rock Professor of Business Administration at the Harvard Business School. He rejoined the Harvard Business School faculty in January, 1982, having previously served as a member of the faculty and research staff from 1966–1978. Professor Stevenson received a B.S. in Mathematics from Stanford and M.B.A. and D.B.A. degrees from Harvard. He is currently a Director of Eastern Realty Investment Corporation; Perini Investment Properties, Inc.; and Arbor Health Care Inc. He is a Director and member of the Investment Committee for The Baupost Group, Inc., and trustee for several individual trusts. He has served as trustee and member of the audit and investment committee of Connecticut General Realty and Mortgage Investors, as Vice President Finance and Administration and Director of Preco Corporation, Director of Wolfe Industries, and trustee and member of the Executive Committee of Realty Income Trust. He has been a consultant for private and government organizations. Dr. Stevenson's publications include two books, *New Business Ventures and the Entrepreneur* and *Policy Formulation and Administration*, as well as numerous working papers and articles in such journals as *Harvard Business Review, Urban Land, Journal of Real Estate Taxation, Real Estate Review,* and *Sloan Management Review.*

William E. Wetzel, Jr., is Professor of Business Administration at the Whittemore School of Business and Economics at the University of New Hampshire. Professor Wetzel's professional and research interests include the role of the entrepreneur in economic development, the financial management of dynamic small firms, and the informal risk capital markets. He has authored articles published in the *New England Journal of Business and Economics, Business Horizons, Black Enterprise, Sloan Management Review, Technovation, Journal of Minority Business Finance, Pratt's Guide to Venture Capital Sources, The Encyclopedia of Entrepreneurship, Venture's Guide to Investing in Private Companies, In Business,* and others. Professor Wetzel serves on the Board of Directors of BankEast Corporation, DICE Systems Inc., and Craig Supply Company Inc. He also serves on the Board of Directors of Venture Capital Network Inc., the Small Business High Technology Council of New Hampshire, and the Smaller Business Association of New England.

About the Editor

Robert D. Hisrich is the Bovaird Chair Professor of Entrepreneurial Studies and Private Enterprise and Professor of Marketing at The University of Tulsa. He is also President of H & P Associates, a marketing and management consulting firm that he founded. He has previously served on the faculties of Boston College, the Massachusetts Institute of Technology, the National Institute for Higher Education (Ireland), and the University of Puerto Rico. Dr. Hisrich holds degrees from DePauw University and the University of Cincinnati. He spent several years in line and staff positions at Proctor and Gamble and Ford Motor Company. While at Boston College, Dr. Hisrich ran the Small Business Institute, frequently winning the award for the best project in the state and region. He also was instrumental in establishing the Student Agency (a student entrepreneurial corporation) and the Small Business Development Center at the University. He is the author of five books: *The Woman Entrepreneur: Starting, Financing, and Managing a Successful New Business* (coauthored by Candida G. Brush); *Marketing a New Product: Its Planning, Development, and Management; The MBA Center; Marketing Decisions for New and Mature Products; Marketing: A Practical Managerial Approach.* He has authored over fifty articles published in such journals as: *Journal of Marketing, Journal of Marketing Research, International Journal of Business, Sloan Management Review, Columbia Journal of World Business, Journal of Small Business, Leadership and Organization Development Journal, Academy of Management Review,* and *Strategic Management Journal.* Dr. Hisrich has consulted to numerous large and small corporations, founded and operated several successful businesses, and designed and delivered management and entrepreneurial programs to U.S. and foreign businesses and governments. He recently established an Enterprise Development Center at The University of Tulsa for creating new ventures.